Longman

'ress

York Press
322 Old Brompton Road, London SW5 9JH

Pearson Education Limited
Edinburgh Gate, Harlow, Essex CM20 2JE, United Kingdom
Associated companies, branches and representatives throughout
the world

First published 2000

ISBN 0-582-43198-0

Designed by Vicki Pacey
Phototypeset by Gem Graphics, Trenance, Mawgan Porth, Cornwall
Colour reproduction and film output by Spectrum Colour
Printed in Malaysia, KVP

contents

acknowledgements

Thanks to my wife Kirsten for watching all those sci-fi films with me and speaking so intelligently about them and *Blade Runner*.

—///—

author of this note

Nick Lacey graduated from Warwick University in Film/Literature and has been teaching Media Studies since 1990. He is a contributing editor to *in the picture*, a magazine for teachers of media studies. He is author of *Image and Representation* (Macmillan Press), *Narrative and Genre* (Macmillan Press) and *Exam Success Guide: Media Studies* (Philip Allan).

background

trailer

The following reviews of *Blade Runner*, from its original release in 1982 and The 'Director's Cut' in 1992, show the mixed critical response to the film.

> Much to its own detriment, *Blade Runner* is so busy emulating the box-office trumps played by *Star Wars* and *Raiders of the Lost Ark* – respectively, toytown hardware and explosive violence – that its *raison d'être*, alias Philip K. Dick, gets rather lost in the wash.
>
> Tom Milne, Monthly Film Bulletin (Vol. 49, no. 584, September 1982)

> Director Ridley Scott, noted for his elaborate production design on "Alien," again brings to the screen a brilliantly conceived view of the future that falters only when a weak screenplay gets in the way. Thanks to special effects wizards Douglas Trumbull, Richard Yuricich and David Dryer, "Bade [sic] Runner" is a mesmerizing peek into the near future. Set in a horribly polluted Los Angeles teeming with street urchins, the story serves as a device to explore this neon nightmare that is Ridley Scott's vision of things to come.
>
> Box Office, (http://www.boxoffice.com/cgi/classicsearch.pl), August 1982

> I watched the original "Blade Runner" on video a few years ago, and now, watching the director's cut, I am left with the same over-all opinion of the movie: It looks fabulous, it uses special effects to create a new world of its own, but it is thin in its human story. The movie creates a vision of Los Angeles, circa 2020, which is as original and memorable as such other future worlds as Fritz Lang's "Metropolis" or Spielberg's [sic] "Star Wars" planets. Unimaginable skyscrapers tower over streets that are clotted with humanity;

trailer   background

around the skirts of the billion-dollar towers, the city at ground level looks like a third-world bazaar.

Roger Ebert, Chicago Sun-Times,
(http://www.suntimes.com/ebert/ebert_reviews/1992/09/776957.html),
9 November, 1992

The fact is, this movie is great in any version. On the Uptown Theatre's curvaceous, jumbo screen, it will knock your socks off. Personally, I thought the final scene in the 1982 version – featuring borrowed footage from Stanley Kubrick's "The Shining" – was tremendous. After a few viewings of the film, I even grew to like Ford's sluggish, rather superfluous narration. But at the same time, I don't miss what has been cut from the new version. The overall effect is so beautifully wrought, a few details aren't going to bring things crashing down.

Desson Howe, Washington Post 11 September, 1992

reading blade runner

Blade Runner, based on a novel by Philip K. Dick and directed by Ridley Scott, was originally released in 1982 to general critical derision and was a box office failure. In 1982 most viewers were impressed by the astounding vision of the future presented by the film but many were confused by the narrative and assumed it to be incoherent. However, it became a cult movie (see Contexts: Audience) and was eventually re-released as *Blade Runner – The Director's Cut* in 1992. Critical reception was again mixed but the box office, on a restricted release, was relatively good.

Now the film is 'canonised' by *York Film Notes* and the British Film Institute's *Modern Classics* series, it is seen to be an endlessly fascinating movie and one of the few great science fiction films of the twentieth century.

In Britain at least, science fiction (sci-fi) remains in the literary ghetto inhabited by pulp fiction. In bookshops, the genre is corralled on its own – like crime – and the glaring, lurid colours of the books seem to warn off non-anoraks. In North America, however, the genre thrives in academic journals and is recognised as one of the most vibrant areas of literature.

6   BLADE RUNNER

chilling, bold, mesmerizing, futuristic detective thriller

HARRISON FORD is

BLADE RUNNER

JERRY PERENCHIO AND BUD YORKIN PRESENT A MICHAEL DEELEY-RIDLEY SCOTT PRODUCTION
A FILM BY RIDLEY SCOTT
STARRING HARRISON FORD
IN BLADE RUNNER WITH RUTGER HAUER SEAN YOUNG
EDWARD JAMES OLMOS SCREENPLAY BY HAMPTON FANCHER AND DAVID PEOPLES
EXECUTIVE PRODUCERS BRIAN KELLY AND HAMPTON FANCHER VISUAL EFFECTS BY DOUGLAS TRUMBULL
ORIGINAL MUSIC COMPOSED BY VANGELIS PRODUCED BY MICHAEL DEELEY DIRECTED BY RIDLEY SCOTT

Blade Runner: one of the few great science fiction films of the twentieth century. As the poster suggests, its visual conception provides virtually endless visual pleasure.

reading blade runner   background

why is it always dark?

It is probably the 'fantasy' element of sci-fi that puts many off the genre: the belief that it has nothing to say about contemporary life and that its narrative worlds are unbelievable. Certainly much of sci-fi, like all genres, is essentially escapist and, as such, performs an important function. However we must distinguish between these sci-fi texts which are 'non-genre' – or 'soft' – sci-fi, and those which deal with issues concerning what it means to be human which are 'genre' – or 'hard' – sci-fi. Far from escaping everyday life, these texts often lead us into the mire of contemporary existence. Genre sci-fi is never about the future, it is about now.

Blade Runner is genre sci-fi and deals with questions of humanity through a comparison between the replicants – particularly Roy Batty – and their hunter, Deckard. Although the replicants are machines, the film suggests that, in the characters of Batty and Rachael, they have much to teach us about acting like a human being. Although Deckard appears to be the central character, he verges on being an anti-hero in his attitude and actions.

Fans of 'genre' sci-fi are used to considering such issues, just as they are used to creating – through their reading – alien worlds. The critics who complained that they could not make sense of the world of LA 2019 were simply not working hard enough. For example, it is quite easy to infer the answers to the following questions:

■ Why is it always dark?

There has been an ecological disaster that has polluted the atmosphere, virtually obliterating the sun.

■ Why is the city full of 'foreigners'?

Everyone who can has gone 'Off-world' and the races left behind are those who have been economically discriminated against.

■ Why is the language spoken on the street unlike our own?

Language is constantly changing and the cityspeak of LA 2019 is a melange of Japanese, German and Spanish. This evokes the future by combining languages to make the familiar different.

altered states of reality

■ Why are some parts of the city overcrowded and others deserted?
The over-crowding is seen in the market sector; Sebastian's apartment is deserted but who would want to live there?

And so on.

The film's fascination does not simply reside in its philosophy; the extraordinary nature of its visual conception provides virtually endless visual pleasure and presents a well-rounded, convincing view of our future.

Because the film became a cult, obsessive fans have analysed the film frame by frame and shared their conclusions on the internet. In addition, the 'false' ending in the original version provided fuel for much debate during the 1980s which the release of The 'Director's Cut' in 1991 only partially dampened. Discussion of *Blade Runner* is encouraged because it is an open text that allows a wide range of interpretation to be justified from a close reading.

To enjoy *Blade Runner*, you do not have to be a fan of sci-fi, you simply have to be interested in what it means to be human at the beginning of the twenty-first century.

It can be assumed, unless otherwise stated, that this book is referring to The 'Director's Cut' because this is the most satisfying version; this is referred to simply as *Blade Runner*. Any details that are specific to the original version will be mentioned at the time.

key players' biographies

THE NOVELIST: PHILIP K. DICK (1928–1982)

Dick's life was plagued by illness and drug addiction. This may have helped him create the altered states of reality that populate his fictions where we can rarely be sure that what we are seeing can be believed. He also experienced five marriages and divorces, and survived two suicide attempts.

He was an exceedingly prolific writer, mainly for economic reasons. After failing to sell any 'mainstream' fiction, he turned to sci-fi and became one of the great authors in the genre. A good starting place for any reader new to Dick is *The Man in the High Castle* (1962), an 'alternative world' narrative where the axis-powers – Germany and Japan – won the Second World War.

biographies

This novel won sci-fi's Hugo award; his other 'gong' – a John W. Campbell award – was for *Flow My Tears, The Policeman Said* (1974) which, like *Time Out of Joint* (1959), can be seen as a precursor to the film *The Truman Show* (1998). Dick's novels can be read as philosophical treatises on the question of what is real. That he should be published as a 'pulp' writer is indicative of how the mainstream regards sci-fi.

Do Androids Dream of Electric Sheep? (1968) is the basis of *Blade Runner* but is significantly different from the film. As you would expect from a novel, background detail can be narrated directly and so we learn that a nuclear war has caused the ecological disaster that has killed virtually all animals. Deckard is motivated to 'retire' the replicants because he wants to buy a real animal, *the* status symbol of the time. Rachael and Pris are *identical* androids, which causes Deckard problems when he comes to execute the latter, as he had sex with the former. Although Dick's androids are far less human than the film's replicants, his Rachael also has to come to terms with learning she is a machine:

> Androids can't bear children ... Is it a loss? ... I don't really know; I have no way to tell. How does it feel to have a child? How does it feel to be born, for that matter? We're not born; we don't grow up; instead of dying from illness or old age we wear out like ants ... *I'm not alive!* You're not going to bed with a woman. Don't be disappointed; okay?
>
> Philip K. Dick, Do Androids Dream of Electric Sheep?, 1992, p. 146

Dick's Deckard is lost in a loveless marriage and the book ends with Rachael throwing his real goat off the top of his apartment building and he is left only with an artificial toad he found in the desert.

It is only recently that Dick's fiction has been made into film: *Total Recall* (1990), *Screamers* (1995), *Confessions d'Un Barjo* (1996), *Imposter* (1999) and *Minority Report* (2001). So far film makers have found conveying the paranoia of Dick's vision difficult (*Blade Runner*, to an extent, immerses the paranoia); though the lift scene in *Total Recall*, where the Arnold Schwarzenegger character does not know if he is actually there or not, is totally Dickian. Possibly David Cronenberg, who managed a brilliant adaptation of J.G. Ballard's *Crash* (1996), may be the ideal talent to bring Dick's books to the cinema.

biographies

HARRISON FORD (1942–)

In 1982, fresh from blockbuster success in *Raiders of the Lost Ark* (1981), Harrison Ford was a sufficiently big name to open a movie, though even he failed to save *Blade Runner* at the box office. He first made an impact as Han Solo in *Star Wars* (1977, RE 1997) and he has remained one of the few stars who can 'tent pole' (open) a movie.

Stars bring their persona to any role they play. This persona is created not only by the types of characters the star typically plays but also the way stars present themselves, and are presented, in secondary texts such as interviews and profiles.

Ford invariably plays a macho guy who shows a sensitive personality just beneath the surface. Even the headstrong Han Solo did not possess the sort of overbearing masculinity displayed by other 1980s' stars such as Sylvester Stallone and Arnold Schwarzenegger. Occasionally this lack of assertiveness allows him to play diffident characters as in *Working Girl* (1988), where he can only watch the female protagonists (played by Sigourney Weaver and Melanie Griffith) slug it out. Because 'Ford' (the inverted commas signify we are considering his persona and not the real man) does not trade wholly on his masculinity, he is able to play intellectuals as in *Sabrina* (1995) and *The Fugitive* (1993). The latter film is interesting: he plays the wrongly accused Dr Richard Kimble and bumbles around ineffectually for a while behind a beard. His transformation into an action hero, more in keeping with Ford's persona, is signified when he shaves.

We can consider the effect Ford's persona has upon *Blade Runner* from two perspectives: 1982 and now. The former, of course, is more difficult as we have to attempt to shed the knowledge accumulated by 'Ford' from later films; we also have to try and see the film with 1982's eyes. In Ford's case, however, there is probably little difference between the two meanings, as his persona has varied little during his successful career. As we shall see (Narrative & Form: Characters), Ford helps the audience sympathise with Deckard's plight. He brings a vulnerability to the role that would have been beyond Stallone and Schwarzenegger.

a strong personal stamp

director as auteur

The idea of the director being the author of a film originated in François Truffaut's *A Certain Tendency of the French Cinema*, first published in *Cahiers du Cinema* in 1954, which attacked what he called a 'Tradition of Quality'. Truffaut's intent was polemical and the notion of the auteur was not turned into a theory until the publication of Andrew Sarris's *The American Cinema* in the 1960s.

The auteur 'theory' was useful in enabling academics and critics to give legitimacy to their investigation of popular films that had previously been dismissed as 'trash'. Auteurs are directors who put a strong personal stamp on their films, usually through the mise-en-scène. They are contrasted with the metteur-en-scène, the director who merely functions, more or less, at the service of the script. Once acknowledged as auteurs, distinctive Hollywood film makers, such as John Ford and Nicholas Ray, could be acknowledged as great artists and their films given serious discussion.

In such a collaborative medium, there is a certain absurdity in assuming one person is the author of the film. However, there is also no doubt that insights can be gained by comparing films of the same director; just as there can be with novelists. These points are not necessarily contradictory: powerful directors will often write the script, produce the film and always use the same team of collaborators to fulfil their vision.

Although in academic discourse, the 'theory' is now somewhat passé, film marketing has taken it up and virtually all films are prefaced by 'A film by ...'. This is absurd, as most directors' visual style is completely anonymous, but Ridley Scott, more than most other contemporary directors, can lay claim to being an auteur.

Scott's roots are in art direction (for the BBC), and advertising: he created his own company in the late 1960s. It is unsurprising, then, that Scott's movies, like those of his brother Tony, all look great. He has been taken to task for this as if glossy visuals on their own could be a corrupting influence. The charge that Scott's movies are all gloss and no substance, however, is a serious one that, as we shall see, can be satisfactorily answered. This glossy look, derived from advertising, has been one of the defining features of Hollywood production in the last quarter of the

director as auteur

Scott can lay claim to being an auteur

Ridley Scott takes on Harrison Ford
in the making of *Blade Runner* –
more than many other contemporary
directors, Scott can lay claim to being
an auteur.

director as auteur background

twentieth century. Tony Scott can be seen as the epitome of the High Concept movie director with *Top Gun* (1986) and *Enemy of the State* (1998).

Although the script is rarely the most important element of a film, it obviously provides the framework from which Scott produces his visuals. In the work of David Peoples, who co-scripted *Blade Runner*, it is possible to see echoes of the film's themes. He has also written *Unforgiven* (produced in 1992 but written many years earlier), a western starring Clint Eastwood; and *Twelve Monkeys* (1995), a sci-fi film directed by Terry Gilliam. *Unforgiven* has been described as 'veteran manhunter, bullied from retirement, shoots down undeserving fugitives' (Philip Strick, 1992, p. 9) which has obvious similarities to the narrative of *Blade Runner*. *Twelve Monkeys* focuses on the role memory has in our lives, using the metaphor of time travel and a mentally ill protagonist.

Another influence is Dan O'Bannon, who co-wrote the cult sci-fi movie *Dark Star* (1973) and co-scripted Scott's first box office success, *Alien* (1979). O'Bannon also wrote 'The Long Tomorrow' in *Heavy Metal* magazine, a strip that greatly influenced the design of *Blade Runner* (see Style: Set Design and Setting). The strip was co-written by Moebius, the *nom de plume* of Jean Giraud, who also designed the space suits in *Alien*.

Clearly many authorial voices militate against the idea of the 'director as auteur'; however, Scott is the 'controlling voice' in his films. He runs Scott-Free productions, and employs people to realise his vision.

We can use the auteur theory to assess the charges of misogyny that have been made against *Blade Runner*. *Alien*, Scott's first major film (in other words one with the full weight of Hollywood's marketing machine behind it), introduced the iconic Ripley who has since appeared in three further episodes of the franchise. Ripley is a rare character in Hollywood, the strong and charismatic woman of action. Her superiority to men is evident. Scott, however, was criticised for the voyeurism of *Alien*'s final scenes when Ripley strips down to her underwear. But it is arguable that this serves to emphasise her vulnerability particularly when compared to the alien that has not yet been despatched.

His follow-up to *Blade Runner*, *Someone to Watch Over Me* (1987), also emphasises the female over the male; during the climactic battle between the women, the male lead can only watch.

Thelma and Louise (1991) would appear to offer a clear-cut example of Scott's ability to deal with women sympathetically. He used his status in Hollywood to get Callie Khouri's first script made and remained faithful to her vision. This included the controversial ending where the protagonists commit suicide rather than face patriarchal law. This film was something of a departure for Scott, particularly after the gloss of *Someone to Watch Over Me* (1987) and *Black Rain* (1989), because it foregrounded the relationship between two women. *Thelma and Louise* is a sumptuous visual experience which uses the Utah and Colorado landscape as a monumental backdrop to the women's flight for freedom. The landscape represents pre-social nature where patriarchy does not dictate that women have to be defined solely in relation to men.

Thelma and Louise is a road movie, but it is a road to nowhere. At one point the heroines swerve off the road and find themselves surrounded by an oil field with phallically pumping wells. The environment looks alien and the music, even though it is instrumental and not synthesised, segues into the plangent tones of *Blade Runner*; undoubtedly an auteurist touch. Other Scott 'signatures' appear elsewhere: the rain that lashes down periodically, even on occasions accompanied by bright sunlight; the steam that gushes out of streets; the bright lights of the trucks and the truck stops that cast a neon glow throughout the film.

Thelma and Louise, like *Blade Runner*, is about choices and freedom. Deckard's alienation is engendered by his isolated existence; Thelma's by her life as housewife to the childish Darryl; Louise's through the trauma she experienced when raped which makes it difficult for her to commit herself to Jimmy. The couple escape their psychic entrapment but, like Deckard and Rachael, they have nowhere to run.

The film that preceded *Thelma and Louise*, *Black Rain* (1989), has a look that is astonishingly like that of *Blade Runner* and it too deals with alienation. Set in Osaka, Japan, Michael Douglas (whose star persona is one of the most masochistic of contemporary male actors) plays a corrupt cop who learns the dignity of honesty. While its representation of the Japanese is problematic, to say the least (the police need a gung-ho American to show them what to do), the representation of the city is visually stunning. It looks like a clean LA 2019, neon dominates slick and glossy surfaces. After having seen *Blade Runner*, it is quite startling to see the future already exists.

A later film, *G.I. Jane* (1997), once again has a female protagonist who proves herself to be better than the men around her. Although it could be argued that the sexual politics of the film suggest that, in order to compete with a man, a woman must become a man (the Demi Moore character shouts 'Suck my dick!' at a climactic moment), this does not detract from the film's engagement with male misogyny.

Using the auteur perspective we can see that, if anything, Scott's *oeuvre* is strong evidence against the charge that he is sexist. We shall return to the misogyny charge in Ideology: Gender.

Most critics, even if only to disparage him, recognise Scott's ability to make a film look good; less often commented upon is his extraordinary good direction of actors. While the talents of Harvey Keitel, Sigourney Weaver and Susan Sarandon are likely to grace any film they appear in, Scott has also garnered, in *Blade Runner*, 'performances of a lifetime' from Rutger Hauer and Sean Young.

Scott is a cinematic talent who probably chooses projects for their visual potential rather than any desire to comment upon the human condition. However, if his only cinematic legacy was *Blade Runner*, then that alone represents a substantial achievement.

narrative & form

For many years, academics have been searching for a common pattern that exists in most, if not all, narrative texts. They have sought an irreducible structure that will reveal the building blocks of narrative. The project is fraught with controversy and some critics have concluded that the exercise is pointless (for example, David Bordwell, 1988). However, if the theories offer insights into the texts, then they are worth applying whether they actually do reveal a fundamental narrative structure or not.

This section applies the narrative theories of Tzvetan Todorov, Vladimir Propp and Claude Levi-Strauss to *Blade Runner*. Anyone interested in a more in-depth examination of narrative theory can refer to Arthur Asa Berger's *Narratives in Popular Culture, Media, and Everyday Life* (1997), or my own *Narrative and Genre* (2000).

TODOROV

We are used to the idea that stories have a beginning, middle and end. The Bulgarian-born narrative theorist Tzvetan Todorov suggested that this consists of the following cause-effect pattern:

- A state of equilibrium at the outset
- A disruption of the equilibrium by some action
- A recognition that there has been a disruption
- An attempt to repair the disruption
- A reinstatement of the equilibrium

In Todorov's terms, the narrative starts with a situation in which there are no problems. This, however, is soon disrupted; indeed, it can be disrupted the moment the narrative begins. The narrative deals with how the status quo is transformed by the disruption that is, usually, transformed back to an equilibrium. This pattern only describes conventional texts; some texts wilfully break this pattern, for example *The Thin Red Line* (1998).

In some forms, such as television series, the situation at the end of the programme is exactly the same as the beginning. Episodes of *Star Trek*, for example, almost always return us to a situation at the beginning of the episode where the crew of the Starship Enterprise is on its 'continuing mission'; this is necessary for the show to go on again the next week. In film, however, it is more usual for the 'reinstatement' to contain some difference to the opening situation; for example, the main male and female characters may now be a couple.

todorov & blade runner

■ A state of equilibrium at the outset: Los Angeles, 2019

■ A disruption of the equilibrium by some action: a number of replicants escape from an Off-world colony

■ A recognition that there has been a disruption: their escape is discovered

■ An attempt to repair the disruption: Deckard is detailed to 'retire' (exterminate) the escapees

■ A reinstatement of the equilibrium: all the replicants are dead

At first glance it seems as if a one-paragraph synopsis would give us just as much information as applying Todorov's theory. However, if we consider carefully how Todorov's formulation is expressed in *Blade Runner*, then we are on more fertile ground.

In most films, the 'state of equilibrium at the outset' consists of the establishment of a recognisable narrative world, usually contemporary to the audience on its first release. Conventionally this narrative world is shown to be a normal place and the normal, by definition, is the equilibrium.

Contrast this idea with the opening of *Blade Runner*: after the logos of Warner Bros. and The Ladd Company, the credits follow superimposed on a black screen. Despite the lack of images, the black screen in itself helps establish the setting as an exceptionally bleak place. This meaning is anchored, to a degree, by the credit sequence's music which is clearly in a minor key, signifying a negative feeling. Although it is difficult to describe music with words, it strikes me as having an elegiac flavour, something that is certainly in keeping with the melancholic tone of the film. The synthesised nature of the music is also evident, particularly in the way it displays a 'dying fall', where the notes 'slur' downwards. The use of synthesised music often connotes the future.

The credits are followed by an introduction that scrolls up the screen. This informs us of the replicant's role in the twenty-first century and the blade runner's function to destroy any who are illegally on earth. Its tone immediately indicates sympathy with the plight of the replicants. They are described as being 'slave labor'. In addition, a euphemism is used, 'retirement', to describe their execution. This suggests hypocrisy on the part of the state that sanctions the 'special police squads'. Once again music is used expressively. During the introduction's scroll, the music increasingly incorporates industrial-like sounds under-laid by synthesised moans which connote horror (for me they recall the soundtrack of *The Shining*, 1980). The scroll ends and disappears at the top of the frame and is followed by a 'fade in' of the words 'Los Angeles, November, 2019'. This then fades to black.

The relationship between the sound and image track is further emphasised by a harp-like glissando that coincides with the 'fade in' of the first image of *Blade Runner*'s narrative world. The breathtaking view is at once spectacular and hostile: the explosions of the flames are virtually incorporated into the music, making them part of the music's bleak tone. This incorporation is, in part, affected by the fact that while the explosions, which occur some distance away, are heard immediately (something which is impossible given the speed of sound) the spinner's (a flying vehicle) sound both gets louder and increases in frequency as it approaches our viewpoint. The effect of this is that the explosions are heard as part of the accompanying soundtrack whereas the spinners are heard as part of their narrative world.

The flames that punctuate the scene connote the industrial landscape of oil refineries (something we do not expect to see in Los Angeles) and offer a very hostile environment: the 'Hades landscape'. Intercut with this establishing shot are two extreme close-ups of an eye (with a flame reflected in it) which, presumably, belongs to Holden who we soon see looking out of a window as he waits to interrogate Leon. The eye's appearance is enigmatic; it is disembodied and reflects what it is seeing. Similarly, this eye is like that of the audience's as it is reflecting what we are seeing on the screen; it is the eye of spectatorship. Eyes, as we shall in Contexts: Genre – film noir, are an important symbol in the film.

Returning to Todorov's framework, the 'equilibrium' we are offered in *Blade Runner* is nowhere near normality; on the contrary, it is a hellish place, a view of the future that suggests Earth has become a dystopia (see Style: Set Design and Setting). When the equilibrium is the 'normal world', it is likely that most of the audience would like to see the disruption nullified so things can go back to as they were. In *Blade Runner* this assumption is – to say the least – questionable. The setting of the equilibrium is a terrible place which begs the question of what effect the disruption might have: can it get any worse? In a sense, *Blade Runner*'s equilibrium is already a disruption. So the opening of *Blade Runner* immediately breaks our narrative expectation; this unconventionality is also revealed through Propp's ideas.

propp & blade runner

In the 1920s, Russian-born Vladimir Propp isolated the narrative pattern of over 100 Russian folk tales. He drew up a list of 31 functions to describe narrative transformation and, although all texts did not have to include every function, the order in which the functions appeared was invariable. Propp said that the movement from one function to another is caused by the narrative 'spheres of action', which are usually inhabited by characters. For example, the disruption of the equilibrium is caused by the actions of a villain that the hero must negate in order to restore the status quo.

Sphere of action

hero
villain
donor
helper
princess
dispatcher

As we saw in our application of Todorov, the disruption is caused by the

quest to destroy the replicants

arrival of the replicants on Earth; therefore they fulfil the villain function. Deckard, who must eradicate their presence to restore the status quo, is the hero. Rachael saves Deckard when Leon threatens him; thus she is the helper. Tyrell 'gives' Rachael to Deckard and so he acts as the donor. The question of who inhabits the princess function is slightly problematic: Rachael probably fills this sphere of action because she does not know that she is a replicant; however – as we shall see – the same may be true of Deckard.

Sphere of action	Character
hero	Deckard
villain	replicants
donor	Tyrell
helper	Rachael
princess	Rachael and/or Deckard?
dispatcher	Bryant

My application of Propp suggests that the following functions are present in *Blade Runner* (not all of his 31 functions are included); I have been pragmatic in my application which has meant occasionally stretching the categories.

Function	Description
4. reconnaissance	Villain makes attempt to get information.

Leon tries to penetrate the Tyrell Corporation to find out how to increase their life span.

Function	Description
6. trickery	Villain tries to deceive victim.

During his interview, Leon is attempting to conceal from Holden that he is a replicant.

Function	Description
8. villainy	Villain causes harm to a member of the family.

Leon shoots Holden.

Function	Description
9. mediation	Misfortune made known; hero is dispatched.

Bryant summons Deckard and sends him on a quest to destroy the replicants.

Function	Description
10. counteraction	Hero (seeker) agrees to counteraction.

It should be noted that while Deckard agrees to 'counteract', he is blackmailed into doing so.

Function	Description
11. departure	Hero leaves home.

Deckard's first stop on his quest is the Tyrell Corporation.

Function	Description
12. first donor function	Hero tested, receives magical agent or helper.

Here Tyrell tests him as to whether he can determine if Rachael is a replicant. While he is not exactly given Rachael, this contact does lead her to save Deckard later.

13. hero's reaction   Hero reacts to agent or donor.
Normally you would expect a hero's reaction to receiving something to be positive.
Here it is one of disgust with Tyrell because Rachael does not know she is a replicant.

15. spatial change   Hero led to object of search.
The bulk of the film consists of the tracking down and destruction of the replicants.

16. struggle   Hero and villain join in direct combat.
Deckard's final battle with the villain is his confrontation with Roy Batty, the replicants'
leader.

17. branding   Hero is branded.
Batty breaks two of Deckard's fingers in retribution.

18. victory   Villain is defeated.
Virtually all films finish with the defeat of the villain and victory of the hero. Here it is
the hero who is defeated, something that is exceptionally rare (for example, *Se7en*),
and although the villain dies in *Blade Runner*, he also saves the hero.

19. liquidation   Initial misfortune or lack is liquidated.
The equilibrium is restored as all the escaped replicants are dead.

20. return   Hero returns.
By this point in the film, it is clearly possible that Deckard is also a replicant (see
Deckard below) and so has nowhere to go. Even if he is not, then his situation is still
desperate as he can be subject to Bryant's blackmail at any time. However, he returns
to his apartment.

21. pursuit, chase   Hero is pursued.
He returns 'home' only to leave immediately. He 'rescues' Rachael and they are clearly
going 'on the run'. The film ends.

Normally, of course, if the hero is being pursued at this point, he or she will
escape. It is more common for the climax of the film to be the villain's
defeat, followed by a brief episode where the hero's exploits are rewarded.
Most narratives include the final function where the hero and princess get
married, though this is usually transmuted into a heterosexual coupling
and acquisition of wealth.

It was unsurprising that, after disastrous previews, Warner Bros. (see
Contexts: Production History and Hollywood) wanted to modify the film's
ending and so they tagged on Propp's final function. The original version
of *Blade Runner* ends:

31. wedding   Hero is married, ascends the throne.
Rachael and Deckard escape to a better life and she can live for more than four years.

levi-strauss

As we saw, Todorov's theory suggested that there was something badly wrong in the world where the 'statement of equilibrium' consists of a dystopia. A Proppian analysis takes this further by showing that in this world, heroic action – in narrative terms – is not possible: the hero is blackmailed into restoring the equilibrium and the villain saves the hero who ends up on the run himself. The lack of a happy ending – we are only offered a return to the 'dystopian equilibrium' – gives the film its subversive credentials.

Todorov and Propp have shown us how the film breaks narrative conventions but what, then, is the message of *Blade Runner*? Levi-Strauss's theory of binary oppositions can offer some suggestions.

levi-strauss & blade runner

Levi-Strauss suggested that binary oppositions structure our understanding of the world. For example, we cannot understand 'hate' if we have no experience of 'love'; we do not know what it means to be human unless we know what 'inhuman' is and so on. Our life is full of these oppositions, incompatible differences that structure our understanding of the world. It is arguable that one of the functions of narrative is to help reconcile these oppositions to make it easier for us to live with them.

Oppositions in narrative are usually represented by the functions of the hero and villain, the hero representing what the film is deeming to be good and the villain representing evil. In the original *Star Wars* trilogy, these oppositions were personified in the characters of Luke Skywalker and Darth Vader; Luke had to overcome what was evil within him before he could triumph.

There are a number of oppositions present in *Blade Runner* including human/inhuman; organic/inorganic; nature/artifice; reality/illusion; original/ duplicate; life/death. These oppositions are represented, traditionally enough, by the hero and villain:

- Deckard/Batty
- human/inhuman

a thin line between oppositions?

- organic/inorganic
- nature/artifice
- reality/illusion (in the sense that he appears to be human but is not)
- original/duplicate
- life/death (this is their respective states at the end of the film)

Clearly this formulation assumes that Deckard is human, a contention that is highly debatable. Conventionally the oppositions represented by Deckard are deemed to be good, but this is thrown into doubt in *Blade Runner* because the villain saves the hero.

This does not mean, however, that *Blade Runner* is suggesting that Batty's side of the oppositions be privileged over Deckard's. Although Batty becomes a saviour, a few minutes earlier he had callously despatched J.F. Sebastian (his murder of Tyrell, his maker, can be understood as revenge). And Deckard remains a sympathetic character: he is forced into the pursuit of the replicants; he evinced disgust at Rachael's ignorance of her nature and, at the end, is attempting to save her.

The film, then, is ambivalent. Like the blade runners themselves, it traces the thin line that runs through the oppositions. This may seem contradictory: how can there be a thin line between oppositions? Because the text 'refuses' to endorse one side or the other, it runs right down the middle of the oppositions. In doing this, it states – and this is the central theme of the film – that what it means to be human is, to say the least, open to question. Unsurprisingly, this theme is articulated primarily through the characters.

characters

BATTY (RUTGER HAUER)

When the 'bad guys' die at the end of films, this is usually seen as a vindication of the hero's superior moral and physical might. It is rare for it to be a poetic and tragic moment, which Roy Batty's demise is in *Blade Runner*.

Roy ('king'? as in the French *roi*?) Batty (as in 'mad'?) begins conventionally villainous. A 'top of the line' android – the Nexus 6 – he is the leader of a

Batty (Rutger Hauer). By the
end of the film, the villain has
been transformed into a heroic
figure that achieves absolution
by allowing Deckard to live at
the moment of his own death.

characters

implanted memories

group of rebels who are on Earth illegally, having already slaughtered twenty-three people and critically injured the blade runner Holden. He is shown to be callous in his treatment of Chew, the eye maker, and kills his maker, Tyrell, by sticking his thumbs into his eyes. Batty begins as an 'excellent' representative of the 'inhuman' opposition described above; like the cyborg (a machine that is part human) in *The Terminator*, he acts without feeling and with total commitment. Although Batty is not the film's hero, we know both his names; Deckard, by contrast, is known only by his surname, as if he is relatively one-dimensional.

Blade runners hunt Batty but he is also a hunter: he is seeking more life through a meeting with his maker. Replicants are programmed to only have a four-year life span in order to avoid them learning to form emotional responses. In addition, to make it easier to control them, they are given a false past to help them understand any developing emotions. This past consists of implanted memories and leads us to question what is the difference between actual memories and those that are implanted (see Deckard below). In Batty's case, memories have stimulated him to seek more life.

Batty's quest for a meaning to his life is strikingly human. Humanity, mainly through religion, has probably always engaged in a search for an understanding of the 'meaning of life'. This 'humanisation' of the replicants is a crucial difference between the film and its source novel, *Do Androids Dream of Electric Sheep?* In Dick's novel, they are called androids and their status as machines is never in doubt; for example, when Deckard kills Baty (as Dick names him):

> He shot Roy Baty; the big man's corpse lashed about, toppled like an over-stacked collection of separate, brittle entities; it smashed into the kitchen table and carried dishes and flatware down with it. Reflex circuits in the corpse made it twitch and flutter, but it had died; Rick ignored it, not seeing it ...
>
> *Philip K. Dick, Do Androids Dream of Electric Sheep?, 1972, p. 168*

Debates about whether a book is better, or worse, than a film, tend to be fairly sterile. By making the replicants very like humans (hence their name emphasising replication), the film engages in a fascinating investigation into the nature of humanity. Dick's book, however, includes an exploration of religion (Mercerism), a satire on television and speculates about the consequences of a world in which very few animals have survived a nuclear war. Although Dick died just before the film was released, he was apparently very satisfied with the final version of the adaptation.

When Batty finds that his maker cannot give him more than his programmed life span he kills, in a rage, both Tyrell and J.F. Sebastian. As he leaves Tyrell Corporation's 'Mayan pyramid', we are privileged with a point-of-view shot as he looks at the stars, from whence he came, accompanied by a suitably ethereal chorus. There is also a low-angle shot signifying Batty's heroic status; after all, he has just killed the man who made his race slaves. By the film's end, Batty has been transformed into a heroic figure who achieves absolution by allowing Deckard to live as he dies.

After leaving the Tyrell Corporation, Batty returns to the replicants' hideout and finds the bloody corpse of his lover Pris and – knowing he is about to die – engages in the climactic battle with Deckard. At first it appears the battle is about revenge and he plays cat and mouse with Deckard after breaking two of his fingers. Batty emphasises his superior physical prowess by giving the blade runner time to run and goads Deckard to fight. However, when he has won the battle, and Deckard hangs precariously one-handed off the edge of a building, he tells Deckard that it is an experience to live in fear. This echoes Leon's words when he was about to kill Deckard, just before Rachael shoots him, when he says that it is painful to live in fear.

We noted how the introduction at the beginning of the film showed sympathy with the replicants' plight as 'slave labor' and this sympathy is made concrete with Batty's words to Deckard when he says that living in fear is like being a slave. As noted in Background: Reading *Blade Runner*, genre sci-fi is not about the future, and equating the replicants with slaves brings forth the theme of racism. This is ironic given Roy's Aryan features; he looks like a Nazi superman: an *Ubermensch*. The film evokes 'passing' narratives where light-skinned African-American slaves attempted to pass as white (see also Contexts: Race and Social Class).

Batty – the narrative villain – is the hero's doppelganger (see Contexts: Identity). Just before he dies, he *empathises* with Deckard; he understands Deckard's experience and he *feels* for him. There is an extreme close-up of Batty's face, virtually from Deckard's point of view. This is, to all intents and purposes, directed to the audience in an attempt to make us empathise with others who live their lives in fear, whether as slaves or because of their physical circumstances.

This empathy for others, the film suggests, is what gives us humanity and Batty shows Deckard the meaning of life. This film

> makes us feel the pain Roy Batty feels when faced with the knowledge of his approaching death in conjunction with his consciousness of his potentiality for knowledge and accomplishment. We are aware with him of all the valuable things he will never know or do.
>
> *Marilyn Gwaltney in Judith Kerman (ed.), 1997, p. 36*

In another doubling, Batty, like Deckard, is a detective:

> Where Deckard behaves with cynical professional distance, Roy acts from the beginning out of profound personal rage. Where Deckard uses impersonal electronic methods of detection, Batty is always personally confrontational and seems by instinct to know where to be. Roy is never seen in transit as Deckard so often is, but is always shown at the point of arrival.
>
> *Jack Boozer Jr in Judith Kerman (ed.), 1997, p. 220*

Batty dies, releasing the dove of peace, more hero than villain. He has learned the value of life and teaches Deckard its value by saving him.

DECKARD (HARRISON FORD)

Both the director and producer of *Blade Runner* felt that Harrison Ford was the ideal actor to portray 'Deckard's curious mixture of emerging sensitivity and hard-boiled bureaucracy' (Paul Sammon, 1996, p. 88).

characters

Deckard certainly is an ambivalent hero: he is blackmailed into his quest to find and destroy the replicants – thereby demonstrating weakness – and, more significantly, he may even be a replicant.

The question surrounding the ontological status of Deckard is one that has buzzed around the film for many years. In the original version, there was little or no doubt about Deckard's status as a human being. In The 'Director's Cut', however, the insertion of a unicorn 'dream sequence' (see Style: The 'Director's Cut') links with Gaff's origami figure left outside Deckard's apartment at the end to suggest that he too is a replicant. If he were not, then how could Gaff know he had dreamed of a unicorn? There are other clues:

■ Rachael asks Deckard if he has taken the Voigt-Kampff test himself, to which he does not answer

■ Deckard has numerous photographs – which seem to belong to the early years of the twentieth century – on his piano, suggesting a Leon-like obsession

■ His eyes reflect light back when he tells Rachael that someone would pursue her, like the fake owl's and the replicants' eyes

■ Gaff tells Deckard that he has 'done a man's job, sir' after Batty's death; this could be ironic

■ Gaff trails Deckard as if he is his human minder

■ He is unemotional; in the original version, his voice-over tells us his wife called him *sushi* (cold fish)

■ Bryant states that six 'skin jobs' are on the loose and only five are accounted for; Deckard could conceivably be the sixth (the actual sixth replicant was written out and remains in Bryant's speech by mistake, but this fact is irrelevant to our consideration of the film)

■ Deckard and Batty repair their damaged hands in parallel during the climactic battle, thus equating the two

■ Zhora asks him if he is 'for real' when he attempts to enter her dressing room

Deckard's memories of being a blade runner, and indeed of his wife, who has moved Off-world in the original version, could be implanted. However, this begs the question of why Bryant sends a replicant who is physically inferior to the Nexus 6. The unicorn scene can be read differently from meaning that Gaff knows what Deckard's dreams are (see Style: The 'Director's Cut').

Essentially it does not matter whether Deckard is a replicant or not; the point of the film is that to act like a human – to be able to empathise with others – is to be human. If he is a replicant, then the opposition with Batty becomes, to a degree, false: we are no longer being asked to compare the alienated flesh and blood with the technological 'fighter full of life'. The suggestion that Deckard may be a replicant serves to emphasise that the definition of what we understand humans to be is ambiguous.

Blade Runner offers us a narrative hero who kills one woman by shooting her in the back and leaves another thrashing in agony after being disembowelled. Deckard also virtually rapes the film's heroine, Rachael (see Contexts: Gender). As a detective, he does very little detecting and is particularly ineffectual in his attempts to threaten Taffey Lewis into giving the whereabouts of Zhora. He loses his gun more than he uses it. Despite his bravery in the battle with Batty, he is clearly second best and has to rely upon his enemy's mercy. Leon would have killed him if Rachael had not intervened. He also appears to have a fondness for alcohol that leads him, rather pathetically, to invite Rachael for a drink in a seedy part of the city.

Deckard, however, retains our sympathy because:

■ He is played by Harrison Ford, one of the top Hollywood stars who always plays 'good guys'

■ He no longer wishes to hunt replicants, possibly having become convinced of their essential humanity, and has to be blackmailed into the job

■ His penchant for alcohol is understandable in the hellish world in which he lives

■ He obviously feels remorse after killing Zhora and sympathy for Rachael, who is ignorant of her state of being

While Batty moves from being a psychopathic killer to a saviour, his

Deckard prepares to dispatch
another woman: the veil is no
protection against being shot.

double – Deckard – progresses from being a man who has no meaning in his life to one with a purpose: to save and be with his lover, Rachael.

TYRELL (JOE TURKEL)

There are numerous legends about the creation of artificial life and the fear that the creation may turn against humanity. Tyrell is like the eponymous character in Mary Shelley's novel *Frankenstein*: he attempts to usurp God's role as the sole creator of life and is murdered by what he has made. Although Tyrell's role in the narrative is as a 'donor', in terms of the morality of the film he is the true villain.

Tyrell is the generic mad scientist. In *Metropolis*, the mad scientist, Rotwang, on the orders of a capitalist, creates a robot to mislead the masses. In *Blade Runner*, Tyrell is both the scientist and a capitalist whose only concern is profit; he even deals shares in bed.

Although Tyrell gets his comeuppance, capitalists like Tyrell are obviously the wielders of power in 2019: the sun is only seen once and that is from Tyrell's Corporation; the city is infested with advertising blimps whose lights even penetrate the private spaces of home; there is no sense of the State possessing power in the film. Indeed, Tyrell is also represented by religious iconography.

> His bed, pedestaled and canopied, was modeled after the bed of Pope John Paul II. Indeed, Tyrell's ecclesiastical aura stems from the repressed divinity of the technological man, who steals power from the gods (and from women) to give birth on his own.
>
> *Janice Hocker Rushing and Thomas S. Frentz, 1995, p. 148*

His violent death, literally in the hands of Batty, seems just.

RACHAEL (SEAN YOUNG)

Rachael is the equivalent of the *femme fatale* character that inhabits many films noir (see Contexts: Genre – film noir), who often seduces the hero and leads him to a bad end. Her padded shoulders and the design of her hair were fashionable in the 1940s when film noir thrived. However, Rachael takes the hero on a different trajectory: she awakens

Deckard's dormant empathy and thereby makes him feel like a human being.

Unlike the classic *femme fatale*, she does not seduce the hero. Indeed, the seduction scene (if it can be called that) is one of the most disturbing in the film as it borders on rape. This is one of the scenes used in evidence to claim the film is misogynist, because Deckard violently prevents her from leaving and shoves her against a wall; this issue will be dealt with in Contexts: Ideology – gender.

In her dealings with Deckard, at the Tyrell Corporation, she is shown to be assertive and composed. However, once she has acted as Deckard's helper by killing Leon, her strength evaporates. Like conventional films, women are not active characters in *Blade Runner*; for the rest of the movie, Rachael merely serves as a princess for Deckard to save. She functions, in Jungian terms, as Deckard's *anima*, the female part of his psyche. Her love for him gives him a purpose after Batty's death.

LEON (BRION JAMES)

When Holden, in his interrogation which opens the film, asks Leon about his mother, he finds himself 'blown away'. The reason for Leon's anger is twofold: he has been revealed as a replicant by the Voigt-Kampff test and he does not have a mother. Try to imagine an existence without having had a mother. Being born helps give us a sense of history, which we celebrate annually. Replicants are more than orphans because they never had a mother. It is unsurprising that they are childlike in their emotional development, trapped in the bodies of 'superhumans':

> Imagine the frustrated rage of a child expressed in the body of an adult! The android in *Blade Runner* is such a being. No one expects a toddler to have empathy. He [*sic*] is too socially inexperienced. Neither does one expect a toddler to have control over murderous emotions.
>
> *Marilyn Gwaltney in Judith Kerman (ed.), 1997, p. 36*

The Voigt-Kampff test flushes out replicants by looking for emotional response in the eye; when aroused, our pupils often dilate. The close-up of the eye that the Voigt-Kampff apparatus displays enables the blade runner to see emotional response; the bellows on the machine presumably give additional information by capturing pheromones sweated out by the subject.

Although the replicants develop emotions, these are sometimes, in human terms, inappropriate (we hear Leon's heartbeat at a particularly tense moment). This is what the questions reveal.

Despite the unattractiveness of Leon's character, his need for his photographs is touching (these are what lead Deckard to Zhora). Leon's need draws attention to the role of photographs in our lives: they help us reconstruct our memories. Leon's memories are false, ours – we assume – are real; 'assume' because we often forget events or misremember events. Rarely do two people remember the past in exactly the same way.

Rachael shows Deckard a photograph of what she thinks is herself as a child with her mother. Deckard callously (or simply truthfully?) tells her it is Tyrell's niece. Later Deckard examines the photo that Rachael dropped on the floor, when she left convinced of her replicant nature. A point-of-view shot of this photograph suddenly comes to life just before the shot's cut; a potent moment that suggests that photographs are our past life.

ZHORA (JOANNA CASSIDY)

Zhora is a snake woman (see Contexts: Cultural Contexts) who would have killed our (hapless) hero if she were not interrupted. She is then hunted through crowded streets before crashing through plate glass windows in her death throes. Ironically this scene is quite beautiful to look at (see Contexts: Ideology – gender): it is filmed in slow motion with elegaic music on the soundtrack.

The extent to which the replicants are commodities is evident in Zhora's death. She dies in a shop window that is populated by mannequins who are also technologically created humanoids and are designed to display goods for sale. Zhora, however, lies in a pool of blood.

PRIS (DARYL HANNAH)

Pris is a 'pleasure model', a euphemism for prostitute, who plays at being the pathetic waif in order to seduce J.F. Sebastian into letting her into his apartment. She is childlike, a quality often given to the oppressed but also one attributed to 'dumb blondes'; though Pris is clearly only playing dumb.

She says, 'I think, Sebastian, therefore I am.' This expression of individual will, which informs western ideology (see Ian Watt, 1972), was formulated by the philosopher Rene Descartes whose name is echoed in Deckard's. In an attempt to survive Deckard's arrival, Pris disguises herself as a toy – which, as a pleasure model, she basically is – and, when discovered, fights back. However, her repertoire is limited and she attempts to garrotte Deckard with her thighs, highly appropriate given her profession.

She dies in another torrent of blood, thrashing in inhuman agony; all she wanted to do was live.

GAFF (EDWARD JAMES OLMOS)

Gaff, who dogs Deckard's steps throughout the film, is something of an enigma. He says very little and possesses a satanic beard. The film's press kit describes his ambiguous nature:

> Gaff is a man of the future, a multilingual bureaucrat with Oriental skin, Japanese eyes, and blue irises.
>
> *Quoted by William M. Kolb in 'Blade Runner Film Notes'*
> *in Judith Kerman (ed.), 1997, p. 156*

Like J.F. Sebastian, Chew and Tyrell, he is a model-maker; his origami figures seemed designed to irritate Deckard. However, they may also be a commentary on the action (see Style: The 'Director's Cut').

He almost chaperones Deckard, evidence maybe that our hero is a replicant, and at one point hits him hard on his shoulder with his walking stick. The stick is required as Gaff has a limp that hardly seems conducive to being the successful blade runner that the original voice-over suggests he wants to become.

One of the meanings of the word 'gaff' is to 'expose a secret'; maybe that's what his function is when he says, 'It's too bad she won't live. But then again, who does?' The secret is that replicants are really the same as human beings. Or maybe the secret is Deckard's status as a replicant.

style

set design & setting

Despite being universally vilified on its original release, *Blade Runner*'s set design was the one area where the film was critically lauded. Although special effects (SFX) have always been an important part of cinema's attraction, the late 1970s and early 1980s was a period of rapid development that is particularly evident in sci-fi film. Following *Star Wars*, *Star Trek: the Motion Picture* and *Alien*, audiences expected to be wowed by the SFX and *Blade Runner* did not disappoint them.

The 1990s also saw a cycle of ostensibly sci-fi films that traded on the advances in computer-generated images (CGI). In many of these films, however, the use of the sci-fi genre was simply an excuse for fantastic SFX and not an opportunity to investigate what it means to be human.

Blade Runner's set design and setting is put to good use as it creates a completely convincing world that is set in the future. It has become one of the most convincing dystopias ever created in sci-fi. A dystopia is the opposite of a perfect world (utopia); it is a society that has gone wrong. In order for a dystopia to relate to the present, it must be based upon extrapolations of current negative trends. In Dick's novel, the world of 1992 (the book was first published in 1968) had suffered a nuclear war and the fallout had led to the death of almost all animals and genetic mutations in human beings. The environment in the film, however, has no 'back story'; there is no clear reason why LA 2019 is so hellish.

This lack of explanation was criticised by many. Some critics even claimed that it was impossible to make sense of *Blade Runner* unless one had read Dick's novel. To sci-fi aficionados there was no such problem; used to having to create an alien world from clues in texts, it was obvious to them that a world where the sun hardly ever shines, and animals are all but extinct, must have suffered an ecological disaster. This could be, for instance, a consequence of global warming. Other clues that the ecological

set design and setting   style

balance of Earth has been shattered include the fact that J.F. Sebastian suffers from the 'Methuselah Syndrome' causing him to grow old too fast. It is clear from the mise-en-scène that most healthy white (see Contexts: Ideology – Race and Social Class) humans, who can afford to do so, have gone to the Off-world colonies.

Scott described his technique in *Blade Runner* as layering 'a kaleidoscopic accumulation of detail ... in every corner of the frame' (quoted in Scott Bukatman, 1997, p. 10). This can act as a metaphor for the whole film; the accumulated detail is so dense that it offers endless fascination that audiences can strip down, offering new insights and contradictions (see Contexts: Ideology – Identity).

Scott envisaged the city of the future as being a place of overkill: he extrapolated the extremes of contemporary New York and made them the norm. The comic artist Moebius (Jean Giraud), whose work appeared in *Heavy Metal*, particularly influenced his vision, especially the image of the 199th level in *The Long Tomorrow* (Scott Bukatman, 1993). Cinematically the model for *Blade Runner* was Fritz Lang's *Metropolis* whose vision of the future – like *Blade Runner*'s – influenced many representations, including Moebius's, that followed. To render his concepts, Scott employed production designer Laurence G. Paull and Syd Mead, who is credited as a 'visual futurist'. Scott's basic idea for the look of the film was 'retrofitting', where old buildings or machinery are not torn down but updated by simply adding things on to them.

The logic of retrofitting is that, as space runs out in cities, it becomes far too expensive to demolish buildings, so they are simply renewed from the outside. The overall impression given is a city of clutter: streets are teeming with humanity and Deckard's apartment is full of 'kipple', Dick's word for the detritus of modern life (such as junk mail). Seemingly in contradiction with this, parts of the city are deserted and almost derelict, like J.F. Sebastian's home. The ecology of the city itself is out of kilter; it does not make sense.

Sebastian's home, the Bradbury building, is an LA landmark. Its design is Gothic; enormous in dimensions, far too vast for the little man who lives on his own. Like Sebastian, the building appears to be suffering from decrepitude: rain does not just seep in, it pours in and rubble is strewn across the floor.

The mish-mash of architecture created by retrofitting places the set design of *Blade Runner* firmly in the category of postmodernism (see Contexts: Genre – postmodernism):

> The city of *Blade Runner* is not the ultramodern, but the postmodern city. It is not an orderly layout of skyscrapers and ultracomfortable, hypermechanized interiors. Rather, it creates an aesthetic of decay, exposing the dark side of technology, the process of disintegration.
>
> Giuliana Bruno in Annette Kuhn (ed.), 1990, p. 185

Waste is everywhere in the city, Pris even hides amongst the garbage. One of the characteristics of postmodernism is that it recycles objects, signs and practices in such a way that their original meaning is lost: this process is called *bricolage*. This creates a pastiche where the ancient Mayan temples of the Tyrell Corporation inhabit the same city as the Gothic grandeur of the Bradbury apartments. The language of the street is a pastiche of German, Japanese and Spanish. This collection of old and new – the mode of transport, called spinners, are indisputably futuristic – gives a powerful sense that this world is simultaneously very different and very similar to our own. Futures are, like genres, the same but different. *Dark City*, released in 1997, also used a pastiche of architectural design to great effect.

If the pastiche helps convince us that the future could be like this, it does not in itself create the dystopia. In the analysis of the opening sequence (see Narrative & Form: Todorov & *Blade Runner*), we saw that the opening shot establishes a hellish environment with its mix of fire, blackness and music. After Holden's interrogation of Leon, we are introduced to Deckard who is hunched against the incessant rain waiting to eat. Advertising blimps dominate the sky forcing the inhabitants to listen to their persuasive pitches. A series of shot/reverse-shots allow us to see the wonders of the future through Deckard's eyes, thereby setting him up as the focus for our identification. Deckard, at the start, is a lonely and alienated character; a product of this future society that has drowned empathy in commerce.

While the design of *Blade Runner* is obviously futuristic, it is also rooted in the past of 1940s' films noir:

> This is a *dark city* of mean streets, moral ambiguities and an air of irresolution. *Blade Runner*'s Los Angeles exemplifies the failure of the rational city envisioned by urban planners and science fiction creators, and it also recalls, by implication, the air of masculine crisis that undergirded film noir.
>
> Scott Bukatman, 1997, p. 50

The issues associated with film noir will be considered in Contexts: Genre – film noir.

lighting

The lighting in the film is expressionist throughout; after all, there is barely any natural light. Blue light infuses the opening interrogation scene, giving it a cool, sterile look. This blue lighting is, arguably, iconographic of Hollywood's High Concept film where it suffuses any scene that threatens to look drab.

The warm luminosity that infuses Tyrell's office gives it an almost religious grandeur. The whole design is outsize, like some temple created to worship the gods. Indeed, it is only here that we see the sun in the whole of the film.

Deckard's apartment, his refuge that is cluttered with old photographs and books, is full of dark shadows. Strong back-lighting appears to be sourced from advertising blimps and prying police spinners. This casts characters as silhouettes, making it difficult to read the faces of both Deckard and Rachael as they joust over whether she is human or not.

This lighting scheme is typical of film noir where the standard tripartite system is unbalanced. Conventional filming requires a key light – usually at 45 degrees to the subject – that casts the main light, a fill, which softens any shadows cast by the key light, and back light that helps differentiate the subject from the background. Films noir often dispense with the fill lighting in order to revel in the shadows. In Deckard's apartment, Scott even eschews key light, deliberately leaving the viewer straining to see.

cinematography

Cinema is both about spectatorship (it needs an audience) and spectacle (the audience needs something to see). Seeing, in cinema, is epistemological; that is, vision supplies us with most of our knowledge (see Contexts: Genre). Virtually all films are mediated by the art of cinematography: a mixture of lighting, focus, colour, movement, framing and film stock. Without the artistry of Jordan Cronenweth, the director of photography, the dystopia described above would not have appeared in all its perverted splendour.

One of the difficulties in filming a film noir is to give a sense of claustrophobic blackness without overwhelming the audience. In addition, *Blade Runner* required a lot of bright neon to signify that these city streets are the main streets and not simply a derelict and dingy part of town. As noted above, the lighting is highly stylised: Scott is not attempting to give an everyday realist look to the film.

Blade Runner is shot in widescreen format of 2.35:1, obviously much wider than the standard 1.85:1. The spectacle of the film requires this breadth and so is even more diminished if viewed on standard-size televisions. Although high definition and digital television promise a higher standard of picture, at the time of writing the only place to see films properly is in the cinema.

There appears to be a growing understanding, amongst video distributors and broadcasters, that to show widescreen films in a pan and scan format is to diminish the experience considerably. Sometimes the mise-en-scène does not make sense as a character being spoken to 'disappears' off screen. However, it has been argued that directors understand that more people will see their films on television than in the cinema:

> [In] *Blade Runner* (1982) ... the edges of the widescreen film are frequently filled with images and objects relating to the film's concern with simulacra of one kind or another [though] these images and objects often disappear when the film is panned and scanned ... the configurations in which the principal characters and their actions have been placed remain intact.
>
> Steve Neale in Steve Neale and Murray Smith (eds), 1998, p. 135

special effects

Blade Runner's spectacle is only breathtaking because of the success of the special effects (SFX). The advent of computer-generated images (CGI) has meant that the only limit to what can be shown in film is the film maker's imagination. The SFX in *Blade Runner*, however, use very different techniques that combine front projection, motion-control cameras, matte photography and the use of models. These devices use tricks of perspective to create a realistic vision.

The SFX were created by the EEG (Electronic Effects Group) run by Douglas Trumbull and Richard Yuricich. Trumbull is renowned in the SFX field, most famously for his work in *2001: A Space Odyssey* (1968); he has also directed two fascinating sci-fi movies *Silent Running* (1971) and *Brainstorm* (1983). Trumbull started working on *Brainstorm* during the production of *Blade Runner* and so David Dreyer replaced him; Trumbull then acted as a consultant only for the remainder of the film. Trumbull gave up Hollywood because he felt that *Brainstorm* had been mishandled by MGM. Now he concentrates on theme parks and is a director of the large film format IMAX Corporation.

the 'director's cut'

The production history of the film is dealt with in Contexts: Production History and Hollywood. Here we shall briefly consider the differences between the original version released in 1982 and the so-called 'director's cut' ten years later.

When we refer to particular films there is usually no, or very little, ambiguity about what is being referred to. Once created, most are immutable artefacts. Increasingly though, in recent years, the idea of a 'finished film' has become more problematic as 'director's cuts' are often released. Some films even have material added after the original release (for example, *Close Encounters of the Third Kind – Special Edition* (1980) – which also took material out – and *Star Wars: A New Hope* (RE: 1997)). In most cases, the 'director's cut' is merely a marketing ploy which will no doubt increase with DVD's ability to contain numerous versions.

the 'director's cut'

Blade Runner now exists as two distinct texts: the first version released in 1982 and The 'Director's Cut', released in 1992. The differences between the two films are significant, the most obvious being the jettisoned voice-over that made explicit much that is implicit. The voice-over works well as a film noir device and, though many have derided it, I do not think it detracts much from the film. More significantly is the change to the ending and the insertion of a short sequence featuring a unicorn.

In 1982, Deckard and Rachael are allowed Hollywood's 'happy ever after' as the voice-over tells us that Rachael is special – she has no termination date. Instead of the bleakness of a black screen that leaves the protagonists in a lift that cannot take them to safety, we have a montage of stunningly beautiful landscapes that, it is implied, Rachael and Deckard are escaping to. This is bizarre when contrasted with the Hades landscape of the film's opening; indeed it was added at the insistence of studio executives, nervous of preview audiences' negative reactions to the film. The audience is left asking: Where has all this beautiful landscape come from (actually outtakes from *The Shining*) and why would anyone want to live in LA if the natural world still existed elsewhere?

On one level the original ending is simply laughable, but at the time – maybe as a result of loving the film so much – I remember making a reading that incorporated the absurdity. The film was clearly about how love can give meaning to life and so, it seemed to me, the ending that suggested Rachael had no termination date simply reinforced the parallels between the protagonists' situation and that of most people in our world. As Deckard says: 'I didn't know how long we had together, who does?' The landscape that accompanies their escape then becomes a reminder of the beauty of our world that we are now in the process of obliterating, by upsetting the ecological balance of the world through pollution and destroying essential areas such as rainforests.

The unicorn is an important piece of evidence in the debate as to whether Deckard is a replicant or not (see Narrative & Form: Characters – Deckard). It is usually read as being a dream Deckard is experiencing as he slumps on the piano and therefore he must be a replicant as the only way Gaff can know his dreams is if they have been implanted. However, the sequence is

the 'director's cut'

not signified as a dream in any way; there is no dissolve or strumming of harps that connotes a shift in consciousness, through the use of continuity editing. The unicorn sequence is simply inter-cut with Deckard who, while clearly in a reverie, does not appear to be asleep.

The significance of the unicorn can be read differently. Gaff creates three figures out of paper throughout the film. The first, a chicken, is a comment on Deckard's initial refusal to pursue the replicants; Gaff is mocking Deckard's masculinity. The second is also a direct reference to manhood: while Deckard searches Leon's hotel room, Gaff fashions a stick man with an erect penis. This suggests that, in his hunt (see Contexts: Cultural Contexts), Deckard is proving his manhood. Finally, the unicorn appears when Deckard is fleeing with Rachael. The unicorn is a mythical beast that can only be tamed by a virgin, the single horn being an obviously phallic symbol. Rachael is a virgin and she tames the hunter Deckard, giving a meaning to his alienated life. (The original unicorn footage had been lost and the segment was culled, for The 'Director's Cut', from *Legend*, directed by Ridley Scott and released in 1985.)

From this perspective, the insertion of the unicorn sequence becomes a comment on Deckard's character. This is certainly not classical Hollywood style, it derives more from the montage techniques practised by Sergei Eisenstein in the Soviet Union of the 1920s. It is overt symbolism.

William M. Kolb (in 'Reconstructing the Director's Cut' in Judith Kerman (ed.), 1997) has shown how the preparation of The 'Director's Cut' was rushed and indeed this version is not what Scott intended. For example, a scene where Deckard visits Holden in hospital was missing. No matter, it is superior to the original and stands as one of the few genuinely subversive films that Hollywood has produced in the last 20 years.

contexts

ideology

The task of the film student is to unstitch the binding of rhetoric that often attempts to conceal the ideological nature of a film. Some films are openly ideological: the films of Jean-Luc Godard, for instance, which include the sci-fi *Alphaville* (1965). Genre films – because they are by definition conventional in form – package their ideological message in a style and narrative that usually strives to be transparent. The rhetoric of mainstream cinema attempts to deny its own construction by making it appear that the film is merely mediating – and therefore not constructing – a reality.

As human beings, we cannot escape the dominant ideology that shapes our social reality and the language we speak and think with. *Blade Runner* can be considered in relation to the ideological issues of identity, gender, race and social class, and the time of its production.

IDENTITY

It is only in extreme circumstances – such as the Holocaust or atrocities perpetrated either by terrorists or international corporations (such as the 1984 Union Carbide 'Bhopal disaster' in India) – that we question the nature of humanity. *Blade Runner* does not deal in these extremes, but does ask questions about the identity of human beings through the characters of the replicants.

The first scene of the film shows Leon desperately trying to hide his identity from Holden. Only when confronted with a question about the mother he could never have does he break the pretence and shoot the blade runner. The replicants are doppelgangers, who through their very similarity to us force us to think about our nature and remind us that we are less than perfect. Psychoanalysts argue that individuals feel so guilty

ideology

about flaws in their characters that these are projected on to others. The devil, for instance, is a personification of evil whose function is to represent what we should not be. Traditionally, doppelgangers function as the evil the hero must come to terms with in order to resolve the narrative disruption. In sci-fi, doppelgangers often appear as androids that illustrate an ambiguous feeling about technological advance:

> On the one hand, we view the android or robot with awe and wonder [and] we envy their perfection ... On the other hand [they] are projections of our fears concerning dehumanizing technology run rampant and scientific creations out of control.
>
> *Joseph Francavilla in Judith Kerman (ed.), 1997, p. 7*

The 'uncontrollable machine' narrative articulates these fears of being taken over by our own creation. A double is at the same time identical to and different from us. This difference is the central ambiguity of *Blade Runner*.

As humans, we feel as if we possess free will and we can, within constraints, decide on our own actions. Computers, however, act without a purpose of their own; humans program them. The replicants, because they become just like humans, exist in the gap between the human and the machine and this gap, the film suggests, is as thin as a knife-edge. So Deckard's behaviour at the beginning of the film was more machine-like (he is 'programmed' by Bryant to act against his wishes) than Roy Batty's at the end.

Similarly, it must be remembered that young human beings lack empathy; children do not have the psychological wherewithal to empathise with others. So if to be human is to empathise, what does this suggest about the status of children? The replicants are characterised as child-like. Batty says to Sebastian, 'Ah, gosh. You've really got some nice toys here'; he and Pris kiss passionately and unselfconsciously in front of an embarrassed Sebastian.

Babies, when they are born, are little more than instinctive learning machines. When Batty finds Pris dead, and knows he too is about to die, he howls like a wolf; in Freudian terms he is unleashing his animal side – the id – as he is about to exact revenge on Deckard. Batty even paints his face with Pris's blood; however, he 'grows up' and overcomes his primitive side to save Deckard.

Pris, too, is associated with animals: when she meets Sebastian, out-of-focus lights behind her look like a cat's eyes and the soundtrack 'yowls' as she deceives him. Zhora is a snake woman.

The replicants are not the only doubles in *Blade Runner*. The Off-world colonies are

> like other copies fashioned in this future society ... supposedly better than its own world. Those who remain, consequently, feel much like aliens in their own world.
>
> *J.P. Telotte in Annette Kuhn (ed.), 1990, p. 155*

Batty is not only Deckard's doppelganger. He is also, in the Jungian sense, his shadow: he is everything that Deckard is not. They are brought together in the final battle:

> Batty comes up from the level of the street, a shadowy figure like Deckard's Jungian double, ascending from the subconscious to confront him and demand acknowledgement.
>
> *Leonard G. Heldreth in 'The Cutting Edges of Blade Runner' in Judith Kerman (ed.), 1997, p. 50*

Batty breaks Deckard's fingers thereby rendering his right hand useless, like his own. This unity is also contained in the ambiguous status of Deckard: is he a replicant too? And both he and Batty are assassins 'owned' by the Tyrell Corporation.

As an individual Deckard suffers from alienation, a feeling of angst generated by a belief that life has no meaning. Deckard has chosen not to go Off-world. He remains on a dying planet, like the characters in Brian Aldiss's short story *Last Orders*. His enforced quest to find the rogue replicants leads him to Rachael and he is

> fascinated not by her nature as a copy so much as by the way in which she mirrors something significantly human within him; a loneliness and a longing for others wherewith that loneliness might be overcome.
>
> *J.P. Telotte in Annette Kuhn (ed.), 1990, p. 156*

In Jungian terms, Rachael is the female component of Deckard's psyche, the *anima*. Although Deckard finds a meaning in life, it is one that has little hope of providing lasting happiness. Rachael does not have long to live and, in defying Bryant's orders to 'retire' her, Deckard has made himself an outlaw. The fact that they have nowhere to go is chillingly emphasised with the final shot of the film: the lift door closes, leaving the screen in darkness. Hollywood usually deals in 'happy ever after' (see Narrative & Form: Propp & *Blade Runner*), a myth that only children should be told.

Just before entering the lift, Deckard finds the origami unicorn and remembers Gaff's final words: 'It's too bad she won't live. But then again, who does?' This implies that Gaff has been to the apartment, found Rachael and has chosen not to retire her; maybe Gaff, too, displays empathy at this moment. Although Deckard knows they have nowhere to run, he nods his head in affirmation of Gaff's words which, of course, apply to all of us.

The meaning of life, then, is to empathise, love and be loved. This may be obvious but we do not seem to have learned this lesson in our world where hatred is expressed in the massacre of those who are different.

Batty's quest for identity is different from Deckard's; he goes on an Oedipal journey in order to confront his 'father'. Oedipus, the Greek legend tells us, accidentally killed his father and unwittingly married his mother. Freud used the tale as a metaphor about identity: the male child must assert himself against his father in order to become adult. Batty is returning to his 'father' in order to gain more life and, when Tyrell tells him that 'the facts of life' mean there is no more life, he murders his creator:

> The symbolic staging of this scene indicates that Batty's 'patricide' should be seen also as a regicide or deicide; it is an act of gruesome vengeance against the deified, 'omniscient' corporate father.
>
> *Jack Boozer Jr in Judith Kerman (ed.), 1997, p. 221*

Tyrell is a 'corporate father' because he represents an economic system that commodifies everything and everybody; as Boozer suggests, Batty's act of vengeance is a rebuttal of capitalism. The gruesome attack on the eyes is intended also to

> threaten ... the spectator's privileged voyeurism and figuratively
> threaten ... the viewer's ideological complacency
>
> *(ibid.)*

The film intends the audience to question the morality of a system where the only value is monetary. Because a price cannot be put on empathy, or love, these values have no part to play in a utilitarian economic scheme. *Blade Runner* is investigating how a purely capitalist society creates individual identity and the consequences of this utilitarianism are shown in *Blade Runner*'s hellish dystopia.

In common with most Hollywood products, *Blade Runner* concerns itself primarily with male identity; women are merely present in order to throw the male quest for meaning into relief.

GENDER

It has already been noted that women are characterised, conventionally, as passive in film. However, *Blade Runner* has been singled out for particular vilification. Some of the invective aimed against *Blade Runner* stems from confusion between what the film is representing and what the film suggests should be read into this representation. While there is no doubt that the women in the film are portrayed as sex objects, this does not mean that the film is condoning this sexism.

The way the females are executed has been cited as evidence that the film is misogynist. Zhora's chest explodes in slow motion. This allows us to see the bloody splatter and contemplate, almost at our leisure, her scantily clad body (that had also been displayed in her dressing room). The beautiful Pris tries to strangle Deckard with her thighs and is disembowelled in a welter of blood and writhing agony. Leon, on the other hand, dies suddenly; the only evidence he has been shot is a red spot appearing on his head. Batty dies in peace and although the violence of Leon shooting Holden is apparent, it is as much signified by the blasted coffee cup as the victim's slumped body.

Taking the women's deaths in isolation seems to confirm the charges of misogyny; however, they must be seen in context. Zhora works in a strip joint, the sort of work that is always available to women in the seedy part of town where she is hiding. Deckard claims to be searching for 'Peeping Tom' holes in her dressing room. He tells her, 'you'd be surprised what a guy'd go through to get a glimpse of a beautiful body'. To which Zhora offers the jaundiced reply, 'No, I wouldn't'. The voyeurism inherent in the scene is drawn to the audience's attention.

Zhora uses her sexuality to distract Deckard; she asks him to dry her before attempting to kill him and probably would have succeeded if she had not been interrupted. Deckard then hunts her down through the unconcerned denizens of the streets. Her slow motion death throes through plate glass windows can certainly be read as offering the voyeur an opportunity to enjoy the destruction of a sexy (and sexily dressed) woman, but is this the film's preferred reading?

Scott's shooting of the scene gives it an extraordinary beauty, conferring nobility on Zhora's desperate struggle to survive as she flies through glass. Artificial snow swirls about her, adding to the pathos. The melancholy music connotes tragedy not triumphalism. She lies dead in a shop window surrounded by mannequins; an appropriate epitaph for someone who was created as a commodity.

Of course it is arguable whether this preferred reading is correct but, as discussed in Background: Director as Auteur, there is little in his *oeuvre* to suggest that Scott is sexist.

The characterisation of Pris is entirely in keeping with a society where commodification is king; she is 'A basic pleasure model. The standard item for military clubs in the outer colonies'. *Blade Runner's* vision of the future is bleak and clearly the treatment of women has changed little from today. This is not a case of the film being misogynist; it is representing a misogynist society.

The accusations of sexism surrounding Rachael are harder to counter. When she tries to leave Deckard's apartment, he violently prevents her. He pushes her against the wall and presses against her. Then he makes her say that she wants him.

She is at a loss about what to do and completely subservient to male power. However, the mise-en-scène clearly connotes that Deckard's

Film noir shadows signify that
Deckard's actions are sinister.

behaviour is wrong: the venetian blinds cast shadows across the scene, indicating an upheaval in a classic film noir way. The music, too, from the moment he tries to kiss her, implies that something sinister is going on.

Also this scene can be read as something other than the exercise of male power:

■ Rachael has only just learned that she is not human and her distress means she cannot cope with Deckard's attempt at seduction

■ She does not think of herself as a sexual being; she has no experience of how her body became sexual (machines do not experience puberty)

■ She has no idea what emotions she is feeling, which are presumably of lust if we accept that Rachael does come to love Deckard

■ She is a virgin not simply in sexual terms, but also in terms of her life experience. Her plaintive 'I can't rely on' is the truth.

The sinister music lightens as Rachael appears to reciprocate Deckard's lust and she kisses him with passion; this signifies the end of the disturbance in the scene.

Although the film here is attempting to deal with issues of male control, there is too much 'baggage' involved in Rachael's capitulation. It is too close to the formulation that when a woman says 'no', she really means 'yes'. If the film had demonstrated that Rachael had sex with Deckard against her will, then it would have been an even more powerful statement about alienation. As it stands, the moment the music mellows, the film becomes momentarily misogynist, implying that she is not really saying 'no'.

RACE AND SOCIAL CLASS

Accusations of racism can, to a large extent, be dealt with in the same way as those of sexism. The streets of *Blade Runner* appear to be mostly populated with Orientals and Latinos: Japanese speech and graffiti is heard and seen throughout the film; Spanish films are showing at cinemas. No explanation is offered for this, but we can infer that those who can afford to get Off-world have already done so. Only the exploited are left, whom

Bryant characterises as the 'little people'; indeed, some of the street-dwellers are midgets.

The need for wealth to escape the planet highlights the social inequalities of the class system. As David Desser (1997) suggests, this is reified in the film by the High/Low opposition. Tyrell's temple towers over the landscape; even Deckard's apartment is on the 97th storey:

> The police, representatives of power and authority, spend most of their time in hovercrafts looking down on the city.
>
> *David Desser in Judith Kerman (ed.), 1997, p. 112*

The issues of race and class are brought together in the replicants: they are slaves who try and hide amongst the masses. Indeed, in terms of its representation of race, *Blade Runner* can be seen to be progressive, as the replicant is a

> persecuted being deprived of human rights [which] may reflect our culture's projected guilt over the exploitation, conquest, enslavement, and extermination of other races and nationalities in history: the Aztec Indian, the American Indian, the African slaves, the Jews in World War II, and many more.
>
> *Joseph Francavilla in Judith Kerman (ed.), 1997, p. 9*

The film evokes a 'passing' narrative where escaped slaves attempted to pass for white; the replicants are attempting to pass for human. The Aryan warrior status of Batty is not utilised in fascist terms because he comes to abhor violence. In fact, we can read his whiteness as hyperbolic and

> as the leader of the slave rebellion he actually becomes the deepest embodiment of 'blackness' in the film.
>
> *Scott Bukatman, 1997, p. 76*

Blade Runner is not a reactionary film, in fact it is genuinely subversive in its critique of capitalism. How does a capitalist institution like Hollywood come to produce films that are, in essence, critical of it?

THE 1980s

It is obvious that films cannot be created in a social vacuum, they are always products of their time. As such they both consciously (usually what the film is trying to say, the preferred reading) and unconsciously articulate ideas about their time. The relationship between any film and the society that produces it is always problematic. To suggest that texts simply act as a mirror to the world is an aesthetic that has long lost any credence. We have been examining in this part how *Blade Runner* articulates ideological issues; this section will attempt to put these issues into the context of the early 1980s.

Although Hollywood's prerogative is profitability, thereby making it a capitalist institution, this does not mean all its products will necessarily celebrate the qualities of bourgeois-capitalist ideology. Indeed, even those films that are conservative in their outlook can offer a world view that is contradictory in its nature. In fact they may well be bound to do so because bourgeois ideology itself is riddled with contradictions. For example, bourgeois ideology celebrates individual liberty, yet its prime social unit is the family where the woman is meant to be subordinate to the man.

In *Rollerball* (1975), for example, the dystopia it depicts is totalitarian in nature and the state is shown to abuse the nuclear family unit; it offers a conservative, bourgeois view of 'communism'. However, this is not state totalitarianism but one run by capitalist corporations; so it is also offering a radical critique of the role capitalism has in our lives. Finally, the film legitimises *individual* rebellion, which is a bourgeois formulation.

Hollywood has also produced films that – because of their rarity – are quite stunningly radical. For example, *Under Fire* (1983) and *Salvador* (1986) are heavily critical of the USA's foreign policy; *Boyz N the Hood* (1991) and *Deep Cover* (1992) cast a none too flattering light on race relations. *Blade Runner*, however, is not a film that is critical of the USA per se, but – as we have seen – it is a critique of capitalism's obsession with commodification. As such, the film has dated very little; indeed the issues surrounding genetic engineering have only recently ebbed into the public consciousness. In some ways the film was ahead of its time, which may be one reason why it perplexed many in the 1982 audience.

ideology

Sci-fi is an ideal genre for dealing with explosive contemporary issues because, through dystopias, it can offer a distance between the representation and the world it is commentating upon:

> [Dystopias] are often characterized by radical positions that are too extreme for Hollywood realism. In some respects, the genre that seems most distant from the contemporary world is the one most free to execute accurate descriptions of its operations.
>
> *Michael Ryan and Douglas Kellner in Annette Kuhn (ed.), 1990, p. 254*

Ryan and Kellner suggest that the USA in the 1980s is characterised by a schism between the ultra conservative politics practised by the Reagan administration and the far more liberal beliefs of most of the populace. This apparent embrace of conservatism was probably a reaction against the traumas the nation had suffered during the 1970s: losing the Vietnam war and the Watergate scandal.

Vietnam had been a French colony until a war of independence defeated the European power in 1954. This left the country split in two: the Communist north and North American-backed south. The country then became a 'hot' version of the Cold War that had the USSR and USA at loggerheads. By 1968, around half a million US troops were fighting a war they could not win. Due to bitter opposition to the war, American troops withdrew in 1973 and the north finally conquered, or reunited with, the south in 1976.

Hollywood avoided the conflict, with the exception of 1968's gung-ho *The Green Berets* directed by, and starring, John Wayne. It was not until the war's end that North American cinema began examining the conflict, although *M*A*S*H* and westerns such as *Little Big Man* and *Soldier Blue* – all released in 1970 – criticised the war indirectly. The Oscar-ridden *The Deer Hunter* (1978) exemplifies the ideological confusion that inhabits many Hollywood films: for most of the three hour length, we see the devastating effect war can have on communities and individuals (the Vietcong are merely parodied as cyphers of evil) and the film ends – with no trace of irony that I can detect – with a rendition of 'God Bless America'.

Other films were more direct in their criticism: for example *Coming Home* (1978), *Go Tell the Spartans* (1978) and Oliver Stone's trilogy, *Platoon* (1987), *Born on the Fourth of July* (1989) and *Heaven and Earth* (1993). Dick's novel *Do Androids Dream of Electric Sheep?* was written in response to the Vietnam war: Dick suggests that if you justify killing by dehumanising the enemy (such as those who were characterised as 'Charlie' in the Vietnam war) then you dehumanise yourself into becoming a killing machine, a terminator.

Possibly just as traumatic to the nation as a whole was the Watergate scandal. In 1972, Republicans attempted to bug the opposition Democratic Party's headquarters with the knowledge of the then president Richard Nixon. The scandal rumbled for years and resulted in a number of officials being jailed and Nixon resigning from office to avoid prosecution. The paranoia evoked by such political corruption was apparent in many films of the 1970s including *The Conversation* (1974), *The Parallax View* (1974) and *All the President's Men* (1976) which followed journalists Woodward and Bernstein's attempts to uncover the Watergate scandal. *Blade Runner*, too, evokes this sense of paranoia because it suggests what it means to be human is not simply a question of biology. At the end of the 1990s, 'paranoia' movies have made a come back, including *The Game* (1997), *The X-Files* (1998) and *The Matrix* (1999).

Hollywood and politics almost became one with the election of the Republican Ronald Reagan in 1980. A one-time minor movie star, he became famous as a President who forgot his lines and, when involved in the Iran-Contra scandal in 1986, his memory completely failed him. Despite his buffoonish image, or maybe because of it, the American voters seemed to love him. Reagan became very important for what he represented and his administration, like that of Britain's Prime Minister Thatcher, embraced right wing 'free market' principles that led to the deregulation of many economic sectors; particularly in cross-media ownership.

President Reagan has even had an aesthetic tendency named after him, 'Reaganite entertainment'. Andrew Britton (1986) argued that Hollywood of the 1980s is characterised by a degree of escapism unusual even for itself; this is exemplified by the Boy's Own *Indiana Jones* trilogy. *Blade*

cultural contexts

Runner is one of the Hollywood films Britton lists as working against this comic book vein; others include *Raging Bull* (1980), *Reds* (1981), *Silkwood* (1983) and *The Dead Zone* (1983).

Blade Runner, then, was working against the currents of its time and was, in many ways, ahead of its time; indeed it helped spawn a new sub-genre of sci-fi, cyberpunk (see Contexts: Genre – Cyberpunk). The advertising blimps in the film imply Japanese economic domination; that probably reflected a contemporary American apprehension of losing its status as the world's biggest economy to Japan. This anxiety can also be found in Ridley Scott's *Black Rain* (1989) and *Rising Sun* (1993).

Although *Blade Runner* ran against the currents of its time, it can be comfortably situated within American frontier myths which we look at below.

cultural contexts

NORTH AMERICA AND THE HUNT FOR MEANING

Although it is useful to understand a text's cultural context when making a reading, the paradigms – or frameworks – of understanding that are dominant at the time of the reading will inevitably dominate how the text is understood. Genre is a very powerful cultural context, as we shall see later in this part, but *Blade Runner* needs to be also understood in relation to the myths of North American society and Christianity.

The North American nation is young compared to many in the world, certainly the youngest of any nation that has historically acquired the status of superpower. Scott's *1492 – Conquest of Paradise* (1992) dated the start of western domination of the continent as 500 years ago. The United States were only formally accredited as a nation in 1777, after rebelling against the English, and fought a civil war as late as the 1860s. In the meantime, the indigenous population was mostly slaughtered. This violence became crucial to the 'American experience' and its legacy is still with us:

> The first colonists saw in America an opportunity to generate their fortunes, their spirit, and the power of their church and nation; but

cultural contexts

> the means to that regeneration ultimately became the means of
> violence, and the myth of regeneration through violence became
> the structuring metaphor of the American experience.
>
> *Richard Slotkin, 1973, p. 5*

In *Projecting the Shadow* (1995), a fascinating overview of 'the cyborg
hero in American film', Rushing and Frentz suggest that the hunter
myth – that permeates many cultures and was vital to survival in frontier
America – has lost its meaning in the fragmented, postmodern world.
For the immigrating Puritans, the Native Indians represented the evil in
the wilderness and so hunting them was a divine duty. The Indians
represented the Other, everything the Puritans were not, and the hunt
became a search for the 'ego ideal': in killing the Other, you affirm your
identity.

By the end of the nineteenth century, the frontier had disappeared and
there was no longer any space for pioneers to go. The Beat Generation tried
to flee the stultifying conformity of the 1950s and went 'on the road' (see
Jack Kerouac's novel of that name) and ended up in Mexico (where Thelma
and Louise were headed), a country that often represents a hedonistic
Other for Americans.

Space then became, in the words of Captain James T. Kirk, 'the final
frontier' and indeed many sci-fi texts are 'westerns in space'. In *Blade
Runner*, the replicants are the new pioneers, sent to civilise the new
frontier:

> Emotional creatures of the frontier, living intensely and violently in
> contrast to the drably stifling and exploitive [*sic*] society that
> produced them, with its darkly crowded streets fitfully illuminated
> by electric billboards advertising not only Coca-Cola but also pill-
> popping, the replicants also represent primitive values because
> they are slaves ... and because they are innocent.
>
> *C. Carter Colwell in Judith Kerman (ed.), 1997, p. 127*

In a world of no frontiers, the hunt is redundant, but in North America it
is still psychologically important. Society has yet to divest itself of the

cultural contexts

patriarchal need to prove manhood. This may be sublimated into sport or the hooligan's search for a fight; masculinity is still primarily defined by the physical and by our obsession with technology.

Rushing and Frentz demonstrate how *Blade Runner* articulates this American myth of the hunt. In the technological postmodern world (see below), where humanity has lost contact with its roots, Tyrell represents the pioneer through his technological developments. However, he refuses to accept responsibility for his creations and is 'blissfully unaware of his hubris' (Janice Hocker Rushing and Thomas S. Frentz, 1995, p. 155).

This leads to his death at the hands of his creation, because the replicants' search for meaning in life is also a hunt that leads them to repeat their maker's mistake. Here the full force of the film's religious allegory becomes apparent.

BLADE RUNNER AS RELIGIOUS ALLEGORY

Fiery the Angles rose, & as they rose deep thunder roll'd

Around their shores, indignant burning with the fires of Orc;

William Blake, Penguin, 1958, p. 116–17

The above is not a misquoting of Roy Batty but the source of his words. Crucially Batty's angel (himself in this context) is falling, whereas William Blake's – in *America: A Prophecy* – rise. Satan, the Fallen Angel who dared to challenge God, is the subject of John Milton's epic poem *Paradise Lost* (written in the mid-seventeenth century) which Frankenstein's monster read when learning to read.

After Batty succeeded where Satan failed by killing his maker, he descends the side of Tyrell's Mayan temple, accompanied by a suitably religious-sounding choir (the Mayans were a culture that practised human sacrifice). He looks up to the stars that – impossibly – are moving away from him, as if he were in an ultra-fast spaceship. The shot is symbolic of Batty's Fall; he is moving rapidly away from heaven. He then looks down toward the depths, his face brightly lit symbolising enlightenment; his expression acknowledging the immensity of what he has just done: any chance he had

cultural contexts

of extra life had died with Tyrell. A slow dissolve takes us into a tunnel – which for a moment looks as though it is going into the depths of Earth – to rejoin Deckard in his hunt.

Like Satan, Batty becomes an enemy to humanity at least until the moment he metamorphosises into a saviour:

> If Batty is Satan ... Deckard ... is Adam. At the structural level, Batty's relationship to Deckard is similar to Satan's to Adam. Both Satan and Adam are (or were) favored of God; both are lords of their respective domains, and both may be said to be questioners: Satan in Heaven and Hell, Adam in Eden, seeking to come to terms with their existence.
>
> David Desser in Judith kerman (ed.), 1997, p. 55

There is no doubt that Batty intends to kill the representative Adam as his last act before he dies. The game of 'cat and mouse' he insists on can only have one winner. He cajoles Deckard to fight and, as the battle continues, he is overcome with admiration for this human being that keeps struggling despite having no chance. When Deckard ineffectually belts his head with an iron bar, Batty says 'Yeah, that's the spirit'. He then decides not to kill and collects a dove of peace from an attic.

Deckard desperately jumps from one building to another and finds himself hanging grimly on to the edge of a skyscraper, his hands slowly slipping in the rain. In a moment of contemplation, Batty pauses and folds his arms against his chest, a nail – symbolic of the crucifixion – sticking from his right hand. He then easily jumps across the chasm and looks down on Deckard. We see Batty in close-up from Deckard's viewpoint: a low angle shot that emphasises the replicant's heroism. He reminds Deckard that it is quite an experience to live in fear, and tells him that this is what it is like to be a slave.

Deckard is literally on the edge, about to fall off the blade, and knows – as only someone who is about to die can know – the true value of life. Batty catches him in a superhuman movement. Rutger Haüer speaks his final lines beautifully: the rhythm of his speech falters as he reaches the end (of his life). He says it is time to die.

Batty and Deckard near the climax
of the film. Deckard is on the edge
and about to understand the true
value of life.

more in keeping with hell

Batty's head slumps in a preternaturally slow movement, his head pointing to the left of the frame, as the dove flies up towards symbolic blue sky. A slow dissolve to Deckard's slumped form – to the right – momentarily twins the pair: a final image of unity emphasising their relationship as doubles.

Deckard's Eve is Rachael and, to extend the religious parallel, they are expelled from paradise at the film's end. Many radicals – William Blake among them – hoped that the New World would become a Paradise:

> the idea that the American continent may become the site of a new golden age could be taken seriously in politics ... That hope in turn has been encouraged, from the beginning, by descriptions of the New World as a kind of Virgilian pasture – a land depicted as if it might become the scene, at long last, of a truly successful 'pursuit of happiness'.
>
> *Leo Marx, 1967, p. 74*

Deckard's and Rachael's 'paradise' is more in keeping with hell; as Desser (1997) suggests, Milton's description of the netherworld, in Book One of *Paradise Lost*, is entirely appropriate to *Blade Runner*:

> The dystopia – which echoes Noah's flood with the perpetual teeming rain – of the film shows how far humanity has come from the Paradise of Eden. Batty, as a Christ figure redeems Deckard by giving him back his humanity but cannot create a second paradise; it is too late.
>
> In the film there is no further redemption after the 'Fall'. Redemption comes to Deckard and Rachael from the humanistic idea of transcendence through love amidst one's own existential condition:
>
> 'Humanism', taken at its most literal, is a way of life centered on human interests which asserts that self-realization is attained through reason, a significant philosophy in this film about human facsimiles, about what it means to be human.
>
> *David Desser in Judith Kerman (ed.), 1997, p. 62*

Humanism has no need of God, it simply requires people to empathise with one another.

genre

Blade Runner is palpably science fiction (sci-fi), a genre most can recognise if not appreciate. As was mentioned in Background: Reading *Blade Runner*, the distinctions between 'genre sci-fi' and 'non-genre sci-fi' are lost on most. *Blade Runner* is also a film noir, which is an immensely popular genre with academics and has something of a cult audience. In addition, *Blade Runner* was influential in the creation of cyberpunk, possibly the postmodern genre par excellence.

SCIENCE FICTION

This section deals only with 'genre sci-fi', sci-fi texts that consider what it means to be human. Brian Aldiss, in *Billion Year Spree* (1973), suggests that the first sci-fi novel was Mary Shelley's *Frankenstein* published in 1818. Aldiss's argument is that, although there are many texts that have recognisable sci-fi elements before this, Shelley was the first to be based on scientific principles. Like *Frankenstein, Blade Runner* is concerned with the creation of artificial life.

Despite being often categorised as fantasy, sci-fi has a long tradition of social criticism. H.G. Wells's seminal novella, *The Time Machine* (published in 1895), applies Darwinian evolution to late nineteenth century Victorian society. He sees the exploited working classes becoming the monstrous Morlocks and the effete middle classes the pathetic Eloi. More recently, Ursula Le Guin's *The Word for World is Forest* (1972) criticised US involvement in the Vietnam war.

Sci-fi is a genre that flourishes most in literature. This is primarily due to the industrial constraints: novels are relatively cheap to produce; most films need a mass audience to be profitable and sci-fi is often expensive to make because of the special effects. Books therefore can be much more ambitious in how they deal with questions of humanity.

Sci-fi is a particularly North American genre and so it is unsurprising that most sci-fi films are produced in Hollywood, a conservative institution. This obviously militates against the creation of ambitious philosophical tropes on the nature of humanity because their audience appeal is likely to be limited. That said, 'genre sci-fi' has undergone something of a renaissance recently in Hollywood.

Of early sci-fi films, the most influential on the design of *Blade Runner* is undoubtedly *Metropolis* (1926). The earlier, silent film's city of the future is an exaggerated Manhattan where skyscrapers tower above both aircraft (biplanes!) and suspended roadways. Oppressed workers are dehumanised by their repetitive work – referring to Henry Ford's methods of mass production – and live in the city's depths. The owners of the means of production, the capitalists, have penthouse apartments and a life of leisure. The narrative deals with a class war where the mad scientist, Rotwang, creates a robot which takes the place of Maria, the worker's would-be saviour. The film ends with the capitalist's son saving Maria and a new alliance is forged between the workers and their oppressors.

Although, inevitably, the film looks dated now, many of its visuals are still very impressive. The director, Fritz Lang, was an expressionist and the film has a highly stylised mise-en-scène: workers tramp in unison to work, in blocks, with heads bowed; the factory is a cacophony of inhuman rhythm (quite an achievement in a silent film); Maria is terrorised by a single light source. As Douglas Kellner suggests, the film's emphasis

> on the degraded, alienating city parallels that of expressionist 'street films' taken together. Thus one could read *Blade Runner* as a reprise of Lang's vision of a futuristic city, featuring a final combat which conspicuously does not repeat *Metropolis'* appeal for class collaboration.
>
> *Douglas Kellner et al., 1984, p. 6*

This expressionist design was influential in the formation of film noir.

FILM NOIR

Many German émigré directors, fleeing the Nazis, made their living directing Hollywood B-movies during the 1940s. Expressionist techniques, best used to represent the urban landscape where society is fraying at its edges, met conventional Hollywood and film noir was created. Film noir mise-en-scène is characterised by disturbance executed by the use of extreme camera angles and/or unbalanced composition. The lighting

genre

trades on extremes between light and dark with little in between. Shadows cast 'chains' on to the characters and good does not necessarily triumph over evil (see Style: Lighting). Doppelgangers are sometimes used to raise issues of identity (see Ideology: Identity above).

The voice-over used in the original version of *Blade Runner* derives from such film noir movies as *Farewell, My Lovely* (1945), *Detour* (1945) and *The Lady from Shanghai* (1946). The conventional protagonist of films noir is an alienated male, a drifter or private eye detective. He treads the line between respectable society and the corruption of the underworld, acting as our guide to a sleazy world most of us know little about. In his search for truth, he usually stumbles upon something that he should not know about. The character of the *femme fatale*, often a sexually voracious woman who destroys herself and the protagonist, also populates these films.

Casting *Blade Runner* as a film noir is entirely appropriate. Deckard is a lone detective who is sick of his job and the society that forces him to 'retire' replicants. He is attracted to Rachael, the *femme fatale*, and becomes – at the end of the film – an outlaw. His search for the replicants becomes a search for himself as he confronts the existential angst of trying to know who he is. The scene where Deckard pretends to be a member of the Confidential Committee on Moral Abuses, in Zhora's dressing room, is an allusion to *The Big Sleep* (1946), which is based on a Raymond Chandler novel featuring the classic hard-boiled detective, Philip Marlowe. Rachael's clothing and coiffure are also direct references to film noir of the 1940s.

Deckard's quest, in the end, is not to find the replicants but to detect empathy within himself; this quest melds the private eye thriller with sci-fi. One of the central themes of *Blade Runner* is seeing: the third shot of the film is an extreme close-up of an eye surveying all before it. As in so many other areas, *Blade Runner* breaks convention in its 'contract' with the viewing public:

> the more we see, the more our uncertainty grows. Its world features a profusion of simulations: synthetic animals, giant viewscreens, replicants, memory implants and faked photos are only some of them. Vision is no guarantee of truth, and the film's complexity encourages us to rethink our assumptions about

> perception by reminding us that, like memory, vision is more than
> a given, 'natural' process. There *is* no nature in *Blade Runner*.
>
> Scott Bukatman, 1997, p. 11

Frederic Jameson (1982) has argued that Raymond Chandler's novels allow us to observe the 'intolerable spaces' of Southern California. Similarly, the even more 'intolerable spaces' of LA 2019 are filtered through the private eye's gaze. However, Scott's layering of the mise-en-scène is so dense that although repeated viewing yields more information, it also leads to confusion: what we see reveals itself, at times, to be contradictory (see Audience below). There are numerous references to seeing in the film:

■ Chew, who created Batty's eyes, is told 'If only you could see what I've seen with your eyes'

■ Batty has difficulty getting to 'see' Tyrell

■ Tyrell wears bottle-thick glasses, indicating both his great intelligence and the fact that he does not see what he has done in creating the replicants

■ Tyrell dies with his eyes poked in, just as Leon was going to do to Deckard (this blindness signifies castration)

■ The Voigt-Kampff test shows extreme close-ups of eyes

■ The artificial owl's eyes reflect light back, as do those of the replicants

Eyes are the 'window to the soul', an interface between our mind and reality. *Blade Runner*'s mise-en-scène is dark, clouded by smog and people. There is too much to see, and yet we have difficulty seeing; besides, we may not want to see everything the film is showing.

CYBERPUNK

Cyberpunk is a subgenre of sci-fi that can find its origins in *Blade Runner*. Cyberpunk is wrapped up in postmodernism and first came to prominence with William Gibson's novel *Neuromancer* (Voyager, 1984). Gibson has acknowledged his debt to *Blade Runner* with its mix of film noir and futuristic sci-fi. Among the precursors of cyberpunk are sci-fi writers J.G. Ballard and Philip K. Dick as well as more mainstream authors such as

William Burroughs and Thomas Pynchon. However, *Blade Runner* is not a cyberpunk text because information technology – which is the crucial space of cyberpunk – makes only a fleeting appearance when Deckard analyses Leon's photograph.

Instead of the mean city streets of film noir, cyberpunk investigates cyberspace: computer-generated virtual reality. It is very much *the* genre of the late twentieth and early twenty-first centuries and its subjects include information technology, genetic engineering, artificial intelligence and the dominance of multinational corporations.

Technological developments can have a traumatic impact on society; look at the Industrial Revolution. The 'second' Industrial Revolution is in the field of information technology; computers are the tools driving forward development in communications and science. Information is the prime global resource for the institutions of the post-capitalist world. It is arguable that postmodernism is the conceptual field which is best equipped to deal with our contemporary technological position.

POSTMODERNISM

Postmodernism is an exceptionally awkward term to define, which may be one of the reasons why it is useful in the attempt to deal with the breaking down of the old paradigms of perception. For example, our relationship with space and time has altered drastically with the recent developments in information technology. Although the Internet has been in existence for over thirty years, it is only recently that the general public have been able to access it in large numbers. From our computers or televisions we can, almost immediately, access any site on the World Wide Web regardless of where it is situated (check out the *Blade Runner* site: http:www.kzsu.stanford.edu/uwi/br/off-world.html). This virtual instantaneity of accessing information means those used to old ideas of space and time can become confused. Written messages, that were primarily carried by 'snail mail', no longer take days to cross the planet; we can access web versions of the day's newspapers anywhere in the world.

Postmodernism deals with this confusion with an eclecticism of reference which eschews any one way of seeing reality; the meta-narratives (ways of explaining everything) of religion, science or political credos hold no sway in the postmodern aesthetic. In addition, the replicants are perfect examples of what postmodern theorist Jean Baudrillard calls 'simulacra': a copy without an original. They are also schizoid which, Jameson (1992) suggests, is characteristic of the postmodern condition: they only live in the present, having little real past and certainly no future.

It should be noted that there are many critics of postmodernism. Postmodernism's eclecticism means it does not have any unifying theory (postmodernists do not want one) and so 'anything goes', which can lead to some contradictory positions being taken up. If everything is relative, with no theoretical foundations, then how do we know that what is being said is relevant to anything?

A subversive subtext to cyberpunk is an implicit critique of capitalism. For example, bourgeois ideology (the value of beliefs of the economic system of capitalism) does not seem to be taking humanity on a trip to a utopia (such as the one envisaged in *2001: A Space Odyssey*), but to a dystopia.

DYSTOPIAS

As was discussed in Style: Set Design and Setting, dystopias are a common creation in sci-fi texts. Kellner et al. (1984) argue that these dystopias were particularly significant in the 1970s and reflected a crisis in 'US ideology'. Dystopias can be ideologically conservative or radical: the former often base their terrible world upon a caricature of socialism while the latter prognosticates the consequences of unbridled capitalism.

For example, *Logan's Run* (1976) concludes with the protagonists escaping from the domed city into the 'natural world'. The collectivism of the city is contrasted negatively with the freedom and individualism of the 'outside world' and the film, conservatively, suggests that

> technology represents artifice as opposed to nature, the mechanical as opposed to the spontaneous ... democratic levelling as opposed to hierarchy derived from individual superiority.
>
> *Michael Ryan and Douglas Kellner in Annette Kuhn (ed.), 1990, p. 58*

For the conservatives, technology represents the triumph of radical change over traditional institutions. The ideological basis of *Logan's Run* becomes

contexts

genre

Advertisements are ubiquitous,
seducing people to consume,
and it is this consumption
that has led to the dystopia.

glaringly apparent when Logan and Jessica, the protagonists, reach the 'freedom' of the natural world. Patriarchy then reasserts itself as Jessica subordinates herself to Logan.

Other conservative dystopias include *THX 1138* (1970) and *Rollerball* (1975). Liberal dystopias include *Silent Running* (1971), *Alien* (1979) and the three *Robocop* films (1987, 1990 and 1993). These films do not display what Ryan and Kellner call the 'technophobia' of conservative creations. Instead, they tend to treat technology as neutral; what is significant in 'liberal' films is *how* technology is used.

In *Blade Runner*, technology is not represented as being inherently negative. In fact, technology and humans are literally united when Deckard and Rachael have sex and it is clear that the ecological disaster has been created by capitalism's *misuse* of technology. Advertisements are ubiquitous, blimps hover just above the surface blaring out temptations, seducing people to consume, and it is this consumption that has led to the dystopia.

RECENT SCI-FI FILMS

Since the unexpected success of *Stargate* (1994), Hollywood has embraced sci-fi as an opportunity to show off the latest special effects. As noted above, most of these films are 'non-genre sci-fi': they use the trappings of the genre but do not deal with issues of humanity. However, a number of these have been brilliant 'genre sci-fi' that offer chilling dystopias, including *The Matrix* (1999), *The Truman Show* (1998), *Dark City* (1997), *Gattaca* (1997) and *Strange Days* (1995). Of these, *Dark City* is closest in conception to *Blade Runner*.

Dark City concerns a group of 'super-being' aliens ('the Strangers') who are examining humanity in an attempt to find out what makes us special; despite their mental and technological prowess, the Strangers are a dying race. At every midnight (though time in the dark city is different to our own) the city changes and its inhabitants' identities are altered without their knowledge. Like *Blade Runner*, the film suggests that memory is exceptionally important to our sense of identity. However, it goes further than this and propounds that the essence of humanity is to be found in our drive to survive.

In *The Matrix*, the world of 1999 is cyberspace, an environment created by artificially intelligent computers to keep humanity happy while we are leached of energy. Ironically, the matrix had first created a utopia for humanity but we were not happy with it. Subversively, the film posits 1999 as a sort of dystopia.

The narrative of the 'uncontrollable machine' is a common one in sci-fi and recently appeared in both the *Terminator* movies (1984 and 1991). *The Matrix* also replays the religious parable evident in the *Terminator* films: *The Matrix*'s Neo (Keanu Reeves) is a Christ-like saviour as is *The Terminator*'s John Connor. *Blade Runner*, too, offers religious imagery (see Blade Runner as Religious Allegory above), which is hardly surprising in a genre dealing with definitions of humanity; religions strive to define our nature and role in life.

Strange Days (inexplicably a complete flop at the box office) is also set in 1999. Its *fin de siecle* vision of 1995 – remember sci-fi is always about the present – presents a dystopia that is mired in problems of law and order. The army is on the streets of LA backing up a heavy police presence. Early in the film, Lenny Nero (who is fiddling while LA burns), the white central protagonist, drives through the city streets observing the near anarchy: a Santa Claus is chased and beaten up; burning cars send smoke billowing everywhere. Like *Blade Runner*, lights penetrate private spaces: in Lenny's apartment, red neon suffuses the scene and blue helicopter searchlights pry through venetian blinds. Also referencing *Blade Runner* is the first shot which is an extreme close-up of an eye.

The central conceit of the film concerns a device – a SQUID – that allows experiences to be recorded as real and played back later. This raises the issue of memory, for if experience can be recorded first hand, rather than photographed or videoed, then memory can become almost redundant. The SQUID is an illegal apparatus and Nero deals on the black market, peddling pornography and 'b and e' (breaking and entering) recordings. The device is characterised as an addictive drug which, over-used, increases paranoia.

Strange Days is immensely ambitious: the narrative thrust of the film concerns the murder of Jeriko 1 (a black civil rights leader) by rogue LAPD elements which is recorded by a SQUID. The 'clip', which falls into Lenny's hands, is potentially incendiary, as there is already a near riot on the streets, and it is New Year's Eve 1999. Lenny is a rather pathetic character obsessed by a *femme fatale* ex-girlfriend, ironically named Faith. He is aided by Mace, a female, black security specialist who, without Lenny realising, is in love with him. However, Lenny's only concern is to get Faith back and he cares little for the race war that seems about to erupt.

In *Blade Runner*, memories are shown to be crucial to our identity as humans. *Strange Days* develops this idea: a symptom of Lenny's obsession with Faith is that he constantly 'plays back' – using the SQUID – the happy times they had. Mace, who is an immensely charismatic and powerful character, eventually loses her temper with him, telling him that memories are 'meant to fade' for a reason.

'Time heals' is a cliché that expresses the process where painful memories fade. If they do not, then our existence could be unbearably painful. By the end of the film, Lenny realises that Mace is right and the chief of police averts the cataclysmic riot. This *deus ex machina* happy ending is certainly at odds with what precedes it and is probably a result of Hollywood insisting on 'happy ever after' in preference to a chilling political statement about race relations in contemporary North America. However, the relationship between the central characters, a white man and black woman, may express the film maker's hope for a future where racial strife is history.

Strange Days also deals with cinema. The opening scene gives us a visceral experience from the point of view of an armed robber, who ends up falling off the top of a building. The director, Kathryn Bigelow, especially designed a camera for this sequence that seems to give us an uninterrupted flow from start to finish. This first person narration is what the SQUID 'clips' provide.

Later, in an incredibly disturbing scene, a prostitute wearing a SQUID is raped and strangled by a man also wearing the device. Simultaneously he is playing back his experience to his victim, thereby doubling her terror: she can see herself being murdered and feel the murderer's pleasure. The whole scene is filmed from the point of view of the rapist, using all of cinema's voyeuristic power. It implicates the audience in the viewing by making us conscious that we are looking at something we do not want to see. Most cinematic scenes of sex and violence distance the audience from the material in such a way that it can become pleasurable; we gain vicarious pleasure from what we know is a representation. However, Bigelow's direction of this scene gives us no such pleasure. We, like the victim, are caught in a loop of seeing the forbidden. *Blade Runner* also alludes to cinema in the characters of the replicants, who, like actors, are programmed (by directors and themselves) for an ephemeral role.

The Truman Show, a big hit when marketed as a 'Jim Carrey movie', suggests that such idealised environments as Seaside in Florida, are in fact dystopias. Truman's desperate attempts to escape his cosseted existence end triumphantly as he exits the dome into darkness. *Gattaca* deals with a future where babies are assessed at birth and assigned roles based upon their genetic make-up. Like *Dark City* and *Blade Runner*, human beings are shown to be able to transcend their (genetic) programme through an unquenchable spirit.

The box office performance of these 'genre sci-fi' films – *The Matrix* (also an action film) and *The Truman Show* (Jim Carrey) excepted – was relatively poor, which does not bode well for their production in the future. For a more detailed examination of sci-fi and film noir, see my *Narrative and Genre* (2000).

FILMOGRAPHY

Sci-fi has featured in cinema since the medium's inception. There follows a selected list of sci-fi films that either influenced *Blade Runner's* visual style or dealt with similar themes. The films are listed chronologically:

The Golem: How He Came into the World (1920)

Metropolis (1927)

Frankenstein (1931)

Things to Come (1936)

Invasion of the Body Snatchers (1955)

Forbidden Planet (1956)

Unearthly Stranger (1963)

Alphaville (1965)

Fahrenheit 451 (1966)

2001: A Space Odyssey (1968)

THX 1138 (1970)

A Clockwork Orange (1971)

Z.P.G. (1971)

Silent Running (1972)

Soylent Green (1973)

Dark Star (1973)

Westworld (1973)

The Terminal Man (1974)

Zardoz (1974)

Rollerball (1975)

The Stepford Wives (1975)

Logan's Run (1976)

Demon Seed (1977)

Invasion of the Body Snatchers (1978)

Alien (1979)

Mad Max (1979)

Star Trek: the Motion Picture (1979)

Escape from New York (1981)

Mad Max 2 (aka *The Road Warrior*) (1981)

Android (1982)

Videodrome (1982)

Blade Runner is an immensely influential film: Scott's dystopian vision of the future has been the touchstone for many subsequent cinematic visions. What follows is a select list of sci-fi films that appear to be influenced by *Blade Runner* in their visual style, or take up the themes of the film.

production history

The Matrix (1999)

The Truman Show (1998)

Dark City (1997)

Gattaca (1997)

Johnny Mnemonic (1995)

Judge Dredd (1995)

Strange Days (1995)

Twelve Monkeys (1995)

Virtuosity (1995)

Body Snatchers (1993)

Demolition Man (1993)

The Lawnmower Man (1992)

Terminator 2: Judgment Day (1991)

Delicatessen (1990)

Hardware (1990)

Total Recall (1990)

Akira (1988)

Robocop (1987) and its two sequels

The Running Man (1987)

The Fly (1986)

Brazil (1985)

The Terminator (1984)

Brainstorm (1983)

production history & Hollywood

Herb Jaffe Associates originally optioned Dick's novel in 1974 but it was not until Brian Kelly picked up the lapsed option in 1977, and brought producer Michael Deeley aboard, that what was to become known as

Blade Runner got started. Deeley, a British producer, had made the well-respected sci-fi film *The Man Who Fell To Earth* (1975) and won an Academy Award for *The Deer Hunter* (1978).

That it took five years for the film to appear on the screen gives an indication of the 'development hell' that plagues most Hollywood productions. During the golden age of the studio system, up to the late 1940s, films would mostly be produced, distributed and exhibited by the major studios. This was a system of 'vertical' integration that allowed the majors to reap profit at every stage of cinema. After the Paramount decrees (competition legislation first filed in 1938) were enforced in 1948, the majors were, more or less, forced to divest themselves of the theatres, which are the most profitable sector of cinema. Unable to guarantee distribution of their films in their theatres, the majors reduced 'production line' film making and this led to a vast increase in the number of independent productions. This anti-trust legislation was reversed in the 1980s; by then, however, the economics of the entertainment industry had changed and there was never going to be a return to the golden age.

By the 1970s, most films were being produced as packages: that is they were pitched to studios for funding in terms of their star(s), the property (script) and (often) the director. Producers had to get the package together before they could get the hoped-for green light. In the meantime, however, if another project the star was involved with got the 'go-ahead', he or she could drop out. The director, who may have signed up because of the presence of the star, could then also drop out and the producer had to begin again.

One of the early directors attached to *Blade Runner* was Robert Mulligan; and one of the studios that expressed an interest was Universal. Ridley Scott had turned down *Blade Runner* in 1979 – he being coveted after his smash sci-fi hit *Alien* – and it was not until 1980, having dropped out of *Dune*, that Scott finally signed up. By the end of the year, with the script development at an impasse, David Peoples was brought in to do rewrites.

Filmways Pictures, which had agreed to finance the film to the tune of $13 million, then dropped out. Eventually a three-way deal was formed involving The Ladd Company, Hong Kong film producer Sir Run-Run Shaw and Tandem Productions.

The total budget became $28 million. The Ladd Company was an independent film producer and put up its portion of the money through Warner Bros., who took domestic distribution rights to the film. Without a distribution deal with one of the majors it is, essentially, impossible to get big-budget finance: there is no point in making a film if no one will show it. Now the major studios consist of Columbia, Disney/Buena Vista, Paramount, Twentieth Century Fox, Universal and Warner Bros.

By the end of the 1990s, the major studios' role had changed again with an emphasis on marketing and distribution; the finance as well as the package for films coming mostly from the independents.

Test previews have become ever more important in the commodification of film. In an attempt to reduce the risk inherent in cultural production, studios preview films and take an audience's response from questionnaires. If the response is not sufficiently positive, the audience's negative points are used to reshoot and/or recut the movie. It is then previewed again. The system is not foolproof: *Sliding Doors* (1998) previewed much better after reshooting and became a relative hit; *Payback*'s (1999) second preview was not liked either, but that too did well at the box office.

Blade Runner's previews took place in Denver, Colorado and Dallas, Texas in March 1982. As Sammon points out, the previews were 'mixed' rather than disastrous; they were negative enough, however, for Warner Bros. to insist on changes, the main ones being the addition of the 'explanatory' voice-over and the changed ending (see Style: The 'Director's Cut').

Blade Runner opened in June 1982 in 1,290 theatres, a wide release at the time but one that pales when compared to the 3,000-plus screens that contemporary blockbusters command when they are first released.

Blade Runner only attained $14 million at the all-important North American box office (this is Sammon's figure; the interactive movie database gives $27 million). That meant, in terms of domestic revenue, the movie was a major flop. The intricacies of movie finance are such that films need to take approximately two and half times their cost at the box office in order to *break even*; this proportion will be greater the more spent on 'p & a' (prints and advertising). Exhibitors first cover their overheads from the gross box office take; after this, distributors have their take. What is left remains profit for the producers: often nothing. Movie making, just for the cinema, is not economically sound. However, the 'ancillary' markets of video, DVD, satellite and cable TV, as well as terrestrial TV, can make a film very profitable.

Despite this failure, the film gained a cult status (see Audience below) and when LA's Fairfax Theatre requested a 70mm (double the normal size, giving a better picture quality) version of *Blade Runner* in 1990 for its classic-film festival, an earlier version, the Workprint, was inadvertently sent. This lacked the voice-over and had the original ending. This version was sufficiently successful at the box office for Warner Bros. to decide to re-release the film as a 'director's cut'.

Although Ridley Scott was involved in the piecing together of the re-release, he was making *1492: Conquest of Paradise* at the time and what became the 'director's cut' is not his definitive version as this was

> determined more by contractual deadlines and available materials than by the director's desires.
>
> *William M. Kolb in 'Reconstructing the Director's Cut'*
> *in Judith Kerman (ed.), 1997, p. 298*

Studio archives are not particularly well kept and it was only a fluke that the Workprint had surfaced in the first place. However, the re-release opened well in fifty-eight theatres, notching up the highest per-screen average of the weekend. Those wishing to know about *Blade Runner*'s genesis in great detail are advised to consult Paul Sammon's *Future Noir: The Making of Blade Runner.*

audience

In Hollywood terms, audiences are merely punters who hopefully will shell out for whatever they are offering. Members of the audience are necessary for a film's existence. A film could be said not to exist if nobody ever sees it, but viewers have no say in the movie's creation, at least until the previews. *Blade Runner* is one of the few movies that has been influenced by audience reaction: its cult status led to the release of The 'Director's Cut' and the obsessive attention paid to the film by fans has unearthed a mine of information.

Before considering this cult status, it is worth remarking that the film was seen as being particularly explicit in its representation of violence. To contemporary eyes, however, this seems strange; the gore in the recent 'teen horror' cycle, such as *Scream* (1996), is far more gruesome. This gives an indication of how audience expectations – and the systems of classification and censorship that tend to follow audience response – change over time. What remains shocking today is the way the hero shoots Zhora in the *back*, her lifeblood exploding from her chest.

The 'uses and gratifications theory' is one of the most useful audience models used in Media Studies. In brief, the theory suggests that audiences use texts for entertainment, information, social interaction and personal identity. Entertainment is often characterised as escapism and although few people would want to escape into the world of *Blade Runner*, the dystopia presented maybe offers a sense that our world is not so bad. *Blade Runner* is not offering information and it never achieved the 'event' blockbuster status that makes it necessary to see some films or you will not know what your peer group is talking about. Personal identity, as we have seen, is clearly the central theme of the film and is important in relation to the film's fan.

Possibly more than any other in literature, sci-fi has a number of associated sub-cultural groups such as *Star Trek*'s Trekkers and fans of the BBC TV series *Doctor Who* and *Blake's Seven*. The Yahoo! UK and Ireland internet search engine yields ninety-four sci-fi conferences and seventy-one sci-fi clubs, a testament of enthusiasm for the genre.

However, as John Tulloch and Henry Jenkins point out, it is necessary to distinguish between fans and enthusiasts who are 'followers':

> fans [are] active participants within fandom [which is] a social, cultural and interpretive [*sic*] institution, and followers [are] audience members who regularly watch and enjoy media programmes but who claim no larger social identity on the basis of this consumption.
>
> *John Tulloch and Henry Jenkins, 1995, p. 23*

audience   contexts

Nicholas Abercrombie and Brian Longhurst have suggested that fans and
enthusiasts are the ends of a continuum in the middle of which is the
cultist:

> Cultists (or subcultists) [make] very explicit attachments to stars or
> to particular programmes and types of programme ... Cultists are
> more organized than fans. They meet each other and circulate
> specialized materials that constitute the nodes of a *network*.
>
> *Nicholas Abercrombie and Brian Longhurst, 1998, pp. 138–9*

Blade Runner has attracted two types of cult audience: the lay and the
academic. The lay audience's love of the film is evident in the number of
websites dedicated to the film. Academics' involvement (of course the two
can be the same) is considered in the following Critical Responses.

'Why should *Blade Runner* have attracted a cult audience?' is a difficult
question to answer. It is probably related to the spectacularly convincing
world Scott and his designers have created. Like J.R.R. Tolkein's books, or
Frank Herbert's *Dune* series, the diegesis is so convincing that it reads like
a place you could visit and thereby has a great presence for the audience.

Any well-made film requires repeated viewing (best done almost
immediately) in order to understand it more fully. It is impossible to absorb
all the information in one sitting. Scott's technique of layering (see Style:
Set Design and Setting) particularly invites repeated viewing which, in turn,
makes the audience an expert on the film. This repeated viewing has
resulted in numerous errors of continuity being found in *Blade Runner*.

Films are always made piecemeal; the same scene may be filmed weeks
apart so the person responsible for continuity must make sure that the
actors and setting look exactly the same. It is likely that many films have
lapses in continuity because there simply is not enough time to make sure
everything is as it should be. But, because *Blade Runner* has had so much
attention, these have been publicly highlighted.

Paul Sammon (1995) has listed twenty-one blunders ranging from the
trivial (the change of the movie titles outside J.F. Sebastian's apartment),
to the (potentially) significant (Bryant says six replicants are missing not
five) (see Narrative & Form: Characters – Deckard). If *Blade Runner* had not

80   BLADE RUNNER

critical responses

become such a cult movie, then most of these discontinuities would never have become widely known. However, these discontinuities actually add to the meaning of the film:

> The questions of self and of relationships between memory and self-knowledge, so critical in the narrative of the film and in Dick's novel, are extended to the film artifact and the viewing audience. The uncertainty of identity ... now seeps into the viewer's relationship to that film ... and to the viewer's own memories.
>
> *Leonard G. Heldreth in*
> *'"Memories ... You're Talkin' About Memories": Re-retrofitting Blade Runner'*
> *in Judith Kerman (ed.), 1997, p. 312*

When seeing the film, at least on the first few occasions, we are often not certain whether we saw Deckard's eyes light up or whether the photograph actually moved. Did we remember correctly that Bryant said there were six replicants? The film suggests that our sense of identity is wrapped up in our memories but, as any student who forgot to hand work in on time will know, memory can be exceptionally elusive. *Blade Runner*, too, is elusive; its questions remain unresolved in an ambiguous but convincing statement of what it means to be human.

critical responses

It was noted, in Background: Director as Auteur, that academic consideration of popular culture became something more than a radical act during the 1960s and 1970s. Previously, only high art was deemed to be worthy of aesthetic consideration. There are two other discourses involved in response to films: those of film critics who write or broadcast about new releases, and those of the audience, some of whom may regard the film in cultist's terms (see Audience above).

For Hollywood, the audience is the most important receiver of the film, though most major studios do also produce a prestige product each year that, they hope, will garner good reviews and win Academy Awards. Press coverage is usually only important, to the studios, as potential publicity; indeed, many films overcome bad reviews to register box office success. 1998's *The Avengers* was so bad that the distributors, Warner Bros., refused to screen it for the press. As for the academics, Hollywood does not give a hoot.

We have already noted above, in Genre, that many were confused by the sci-fi elements in the film and rationalised that the problem was in the text and not their inability to make a reading. As we have seen, there is enough evidence available to make sense of *Blade Runner*'s world. So it is ironic that many of the press reviews complained about the fact that Batty was more heroic than Deckard who, they accurately concluded, was a less interesting character. That, of course, is the point.

Press reaction to The 'Director's Cut' was also muted, though slightly more positive. That it was not more welcoming is slightly puzzling, as the now eliminated voice-over and ending were the focus of much criticism in the original.

One area where *Blade Runner* has found fertile critical response has been in academia. The breadth of reference that this book has drawn upon is testament to the intellectual stimulation provided by the film. Amongst the most interesting is Douglas Kellner et al's *Blade Runner: A Diagnostic Technique* (1984), Scott Bukatman's *Blade Runner* (1997) and Judith Kerman's collection *Retrofitting Blade Runner* (1997).

Part of *Blade Runner*'s attraction is its status as a postmodern text (see above) that to an extent became the dominant aesthetic of the 1990s. The very elusiveness of *Blade Runner* is seen as an intelligent reaction to the modern condition.

In mainstream discourse, *Blade Runner*'s reputation is as a classic sci-fi movie and it is placed in this particular canon alongside *Metropolis* and *2001: A Space Odyssey*; a place it certainly deserves.

bibliography

general film

Altman, Rick, *Film Genre,*
BFI, 1999
  Detailed exploration of film genres

Bordwell, David, *Narration in the Fiction Film,* Routledge, 1985
  A detailed study of narrative theory and structures

– – –, Staiger, Janet & Thompson, Kristin, *The Classical Hollywood Cinema: Film Style & Mode of Production to 1960,* Routledge, 1985; pbk 1995
  An authoritative study of cinema as institution, it covers film style and production

– – – & Thompson, Kristin, *Film Art,* McGraw-Hill, 4th edn, 1993
  An introduction to film aesthetics for the non-specialist

Branson, Gill & Stafford, Roy, *The Media Studies Handbook,* Routledge, 1996

Buckland, Warren, *Teach Yourself Film Studies,* Hodder & Stoughton, 1998
  Very accessible, it gives an overview of key areas in film studies

Cook, Pam (ed.), *The Cinema Book,* BFI, 1994

Corrigan, Tim, *A Short Guide To Writing About Film,* HarperCollins, 1994
  What it says: a practical guide for students

Dyer, Richard, *Stars,* BFI, 1979; pbk Indiana University Press, 1998
  A good introduction to the star system

Easthope, Antony, *Classical Film Theory,* Longman, 1993
  A clear overview of recent writing about film theory

Hayward, Susan, *Key Concepts in Cinema Studies,* Routledge, 1996

Hill, John & Gibson, Pamela Church (eds), *The Oxford Guide to Film Studies,* Oxford University Press, 1998
  Wide-ranging standard guide

Lapsley, Robert & Westlake, Michael, *Film Theory: An Introduction,* Manchester University Press, 1994

Maltby, Richard & Craven, Ian, *Hollywood Cinema,* Blackwell, 1995
  A comprehensive work on the Hollywood industry and its products

Mulvey, Laura, 'Visual Pleasure and Narrative Cinema' (1974), in *Visual and Other Pleasures,* Indiana University Press, Bloomington, 1989
  The classic analysis of 'the look' and 'the male gaze' in Hollywood cinema. Also available in numerous other edited collections

Nelmes, Jill (ed.), *Introduction to Film Studies,* Routledge, 1996
  Deals with several national cinemas and key concepts in film study

Nowell-Smith, Geoffrey (ed.), *The Oxford History of World Cinema,* Oxford University Press, 1996
  Hugely detailed and wide-ranging with many features on 'stars'

Thomson, David, *A Biographical Dictionary of the Cinema*,
Secker & Warburg, 1975
Unashamedly driven by personal taste, but often stimulating

Truffaut, François, *Hitchcock*,
Simon & Schuster, 1966,
rev. edn, Touchstone, 1985
Landmark extended interview

Turner, Graeme, *Film as Social Practice*, 2nd edn, Routledge, 1993
Chapter four, 'Film Narrative', discusses structuralist theories of narrative

Wollen, Peter, *Signs and Meaning in the Cinema*,
Viking, 1972
An important study in semiology

Readers should also explore the many relevant websites and journals.
Film Education and *Sight and Sound* are standard reading.

Valuable websites include:

The Internet Movie Database at
http://uk.imdb.com

Screensite at
http://www.tcf.ua.edu/screensite/contents.html

The Media and Communications Site at the University of Aberystwyth at
http://www.aber.ac.uk/~dgc/welcome.html

There are obviously many other university and studio websites which are worth exploring in relation to film studies.

blade runner

Abercrombie, Nicholas and Longhurst, Brian, *Audiences*,
Sage, London, Thousand Oaks and New Delhi, 1998

Aldiss, Brian, *Billion Year Spree*,
Weidenfeld and Nicholson, London, 1973

Aldiss, Brian, *Last Orders*,
Triad/Panther, St Albans, 1979

Allan, Vicky, Gachley, Ben, Geperin, Leslie & James, Nick,
Cloning the future – Science fiction film 1895–1996,
Sight and Sound supplement, 1996

Berger, Arthur Asa,
Narratives in Popular Culture, Media, and Everyday Life, Sage, Thousand Oaks, London and New Delhi, 1997

Blake, William, *William Blake*,
Penguin, Harmondsworth, 1958

Bordwell, David,
ApProppriations and ImProgrieties,
Cinema Journal vol.27 no.3, 1988

Britton, Andrew, *Blissing Out: The Politics of Reaganite Entertainment*,
Movie no.31/32, Winter, 1986

Bukatman, Scott, *Terminal Identity: the Virtual Subject in Post-Modern Science Fiction*, Duke University Press, London and Durham, 1993

Bukatman, Scott, *Blade Runner*,
British Film Institute, London, 1997

Cameron, James, *Strange Days*,
Penguin, London, 1996

Dick, Philip K.,
Do Androids Dream of Electric Sheep?,
Granada, St Albans, 1972

Dick, Philip K., website,
http://www.geocities.com/Area51/ Chamber/1380/dick.html, 1999

Francke, Lizzie, *Script Girls: Women Film Writers in Hollywood*,
British Film Institute, London, 1994

Jameson, Frederic, *Progress vs. Utopia; or, Can We Imagine the Future?*,
Science Fiction Studies vol.9, no.2, 1992

Kellner, Douglas, Leibowitz, Flo and Ryan, Michael,
Blade Runner: A Diagnostic critique,
Jump Cut, no.29, February 1984

Kerman, Judith (ed.),
Retrofitting Blade Runner,
Bowling Green State University Popular Press, Bowling Green, 1997

Kuhn, Annette (ed.), *Alien Zone*,
Verso, London and New York, 1990

Lacey, Nick, *Narrative and Genre*,
Macmillan, Houndmills and London, 2000

Marx, Leo, *The Machine in the Garden: Technology and the Pastoral Ideal in America*,
Oxford University Press, London, Oxford and New York, 1967

Neale, Steve and Smith, Murray (eds),
Contemporary Hollywood Cinema,
Routledge, London and New York, 1998

Rushing, Janice Hocker and Frentz, Thomas S., *Projecting the Shadow: The Cyborg Hero in American Film*,
The University of Chicago Press, Chicago and London, 1995

Ryan, Michael and Kellner, Douglas,
Camera Politica: The Politics and Ideology of Contemporary Hollywood Cinema,
Indiana University Press, Bloomington and Indianapolis, 1990

Sammon, Paul M., *Future Noir: The Making of Blade Runner*,
Orion Media, London, 1996

Slotkin, Richard, *Regeneration Through Violence: The Mythology of the American Frontier, 1600–1860*,
Wesleyan University Press, Middletown, 1973

Strick, Philip,
Blade Runner: Telling the Difference,
Sight and Sound vol.2, issue 8, December 1992

Tulloch, John and Jenkins, Henry,
Science Fiction Audiences: Watching Doctor Who and Star Trek,
Routledge, London and New York, 1995

Watt, Ian, *The Rise of the Novel*,
Pelican, Harmondsworth, 1972

cinematic terms

auteur the notion that a film's director can be considered as its author. By studying directors' output, particular themes and styles can be seen to run through most of their films

composition the way in which the contents of the shot relate to one another. For example, two people of equal status may be framed in such a way that they occupy an equal amount of space; if, however, one dominates the other, the shot may be composed so that one towers over the subordinate

continuity editing the conventional style of editing that strives not to be noticed. There are various rules, for example the 'axis of action' (the 180-degree line) must not be crossed so the cinematic space can be orientated toward the spectator. See also establishing shot

diegesis the narrative world created by the film. Everything that exists in the film's world is part of the diegesis; add-ons, such as credits and music that the characters cannot hear, are non-diegetic

dissolve a type of edit – the transition between one shot and another – where the second shot fades in as the first fades out. They are both momentarily visible to the audience

dominant ideology the system of values and beliefs that dominate society at a particular time. For the past four hundred years, bourgeois ideology has held sway in the western world. These values and beliefs may seem natural, but they are a social construction

establishing shot often the first shot of a scene that allows spectators to see where everything and everybody is. This shot establishes the 'axis of action' (see

continuity editing) that the camera must not cross

High Concept the industry term given to films that can be described in twenty-five words or less. It is characterised by a postmodern self-consciousness in the use of style and stars. Most blockbuster movies are constructed as High Concept films

Hollywood geographically in Los Angeles, however it often refers to a type of film that is characterised by conventional film form and style and that is primarily made in order to make money

iconography a term derived from art criticism. In film studies, it refers to objects associated with particular genres, for example, robots in science fiction

mise-en-scène literally 'in the picture': how the elements within the frame interact in order to create meaning. In the opening sequence of Blade Runner, Leon often dominates Holden in the mise-en-scène, prefiguring the latter's fate

montage a collection of edits often used to quickly describe a journey (like the end of the original Blade Runner). In the terms of Soviet film maker and theorist, Sergei Eisenstein, it refers to a collection of shots that comment upon the action. In the first sense, the montage is usually diegetic (see above); Eisenstein's montage, however, can be a collection of non-diegetic material

pan and scan the technique used to display widescreen films for television's 4:3 dimensions. The frame is too wide to be encompassed, so the camera appears to 'slide' across the frame, allowing audiences to see what is obscured

cinematic terms

star persona how a star appears to the audience. A persona may or may not relate to the real person. Personas are understood primarily from films but also through interviews and articles. Stars tend to have quite similar personalities across their films

shot/reverse-shot a pair of shots in which the second mirrors the first. A dialogue is often filmed this way: the first person is shown at a particular angle, maybe over their shoulder; the following shot is of the second person from the same angle but from their side (their shoulder). This can be repeated a number of times

credits

director
Ridley Scott

producer
Michael Deeley

screenplay
Hampton Fancher and David
Peoples, based on Philip K. Dick's
novel *Do Androids Dream of
Electric Sheep?*

executive producers
Hampton Fancher and Brian Kelly

associate producer
Ivor Powell

**director of
photography**
Jordan Cronenweth

additional photography
Steven Poster and Brian Tufano

editor
Marsha Nakashima

art director
David Snyder

visual futurist
Sid Mead

production design
Lawrence G. Paull

supervising editor
Terry Rawlings

**special photographic
effects**
Douglas Trumbull, Richard Yuricich
and David Dryer

original music
Vangelis

**executive in charge
of production**
C.O. Erikson

production executive
Katherine Haber

costume design
Charles Knode and Michael Kaplan

**unit production
manager**
John W. Rogers

**first assistant
director**
Newt Arnold and
Peter Cornberg

**second assistant
director**
Don Hauer, Morris Chapnick and
Richard Schroer

sound mixer
Bud Alper

boom operator
Eugene Byron Ashbrook

credits

cable person
Beau Baker

set decoration
Linda DeScenna, Leslie Frankenheimer and Thomas L. Roysden

make-up
Shirley L. Padgett and Marvin G. Westmore

visual effects assistant editor
Michael Backauskas

special effects technician
William G. Curtis

special effects foreman
Ken Estes

special effects technicians
Logan Frazee and Steve Galich

miniature design and construction
Bill George

visual effects
Gregory L. McMurry

model maker
George Trimmer

casting
Jane Feinberg and Mike Fenton

stunt co-ordinator
Gary Combs

cast
Rick Deckard – Harrison Ford

Roy Batty – Rutger Hauer

Rachael – Sean Young

Gaff – Edward James Olmos

Bryant – M. Emmet Walsh

Pris – Daryl Hannah

J.F. Sebastian – William Sanderson

Leon – Brion James

Dr Eldon Tyrell – Joe Turkel

Zhora – Joanna Cassidy

Chew – James Hong

Holden – Morgan Paull

Bear – Kevin Thompson

Kaiser – John Edward Allen

Taffey Lewis – Hy Pyke

Cambodian Lady – Kimiko Hiroshige

Sushi Master – Bob Okazaki

Saleslady – Carolyn De Mirjian

Bartender – Leo Gorcey Jr

Bartender – Charles Knapp

Policeman – Steve Pope

Other titles in the series

Other titles available in the York Film Notes series:

Title	ISBN
8½ (otto e mezzo)	0582 40488 6
A bout de souffle	0582 43182 4
Apocalypse Now	0582 43183 2
Battleship Potemkin	0582 40490 8
Casablanca	0582 43201 4
Chinatown	0582 43199 9
Citizen Kane	0582 40493 2
Das Cabinet des Dr Caligari	0582 40494 0
Double Indemnity	0582 43196 4
Dracula	0582 43197 2
Easy Rider	0582 43195 6
Fargo	0582 43193 X
Fear Eats the Soul	0582 43224 3
La Haine	0582 43194 8
Lawrence of Arabia	0582 43192 1
Psycho	0582 43191 3
Pulp Fiction	0582 40510 7
Romeo and Juliet	0582 43189 1
Some Like It Hot	0582 40503 3
Stagecoach	0582 43187 5
Taxi Driver	0582 40506 8
The Full Monty	0582 43181 6
The Godfather	0582 43188 3
The Piano	0582 43190 5
The Searchers	0582 40510 6
The Terminator	0582 43186 7
The Third Man	0582 40511 4
Thelma and Louise	0582 43184 0
Unforgiven	0582 43185 9

Also from York Notes

Also available in the **York Notes** range:

York Notes
The ultimate literature guides for GCSE students (or equivalent levels)

York Notes Advanced
Literature guides for A-level and undergraduate students (or equivalent levels)

York Personal Tutors
Personal tutoring on essential GCSE English and Maths topics

Available from good bookshops.
For full details, please visit our website at www.longman-yorknotes.com

notes

notes

notes